MW01698332

Edith Stadig

Nature's Daily Guide

Notice

This book is intended as a reference volume only, not as a medical manual. The information given here is designed to help you make informed decisions about your health. It is not intended as a substitute for any treatment that may have been prescribed by your doctor. If you suspect that you have a medical problem, we urge you to seek competent medical help.

Gig Harbor, WA 98335
service@rayapublishing.com
www.rayapublishing.com
ISBN 978-0-9854637-8-6
Author and Designer: Edith Stadig.
Originally published in Germany in 2011: "Besser Leben mit dem Mondrhythmus" by Clebitady Verlag in Rutesheim, Germany

Edith Stadig

Nature's Daily Guide

The Influence of the Lunar Cycle

Reference Book

RAYA
PUBLISHING LLC

This book is dedicated to all those who are striving for a sustainable lifestyle in harmony with nature.

Contents

Foreword

"Do you see the moon high above?
Only half of it is visible
but still it's round and beautiful!
Tis this with many things
which we belittle,
'cause our eyes can't see."
Matthias Claudius

Far on the horizon the turquoise ocean water transitions smoothly into deep blue sky. The waves crowned with white foam caps are rolling in rhythmic sets. Now a bigger wave is approaching and I wait for the right moment to throw myself almost headfirst into it. I paddle to gain speed until the wave picks me up and carries me to the shore. I just love the feeling of being carried by the water when body-surfing.

But this doesn't always happen perfectly. Often my coordination is off and I get tumbled in a wave. A lecture from nature to harmonize with the rhythm! Apart from the rhythms of the waves, we can observe many rhythms in nature such as day and night, the seasons, the phases of the moon, and the tides, all of which influence life on earth. Scientists have shown in many studies that plants and animals have an inner sense for time which allows them to synchronize with nature's rhythms.

About 600 different animal and plant species show behavior connected to the moon's phases. Field mice, for example, stay longer in their nests during nights that are lit up by the full moon, hiding from predators which would easily detect them in the brightly shining full moon.

The California grunion (Leuresthes tenuis) spawns on beaches from two to six nights after the full and new moons beginning soon after high tide and continuing for several hours.[1] The Pacific palolo worm (Eunice viridis) and its West Indian relative (E. fucata) exhibit one of the most incredible examples of reproductive behavior linked to the lunar cycle.[2] It occurs twice a year on the neap tides of the last quarter moon in October and November for the Pacific species, and the third quarter moon in June and July for the West Indian species of palolo worm. Biologists in Switzerland have observed the diameter of tree trunks expanding and contracting in connection with the phases of the moon, and they correlate this with changes in the flow of sap in the trunks. A study of 60 beaches in Southern California suggests that water pollution varies with the lunar cycle, reaching the highest levels when tides are ebbing during the new and full moons.[3]

Traditional Chinese Organ Body Clock

Time of Day	Activated Organs
1am – 3am	Liver
3am – 5am	Lungs
5am – 7am	Large Intestine
7am – 9am	Stomach
9am – 11am	Pancreas and Spleen
11am – 1pm	Heart
1pm – 3pm	Small Intestine
3pm – 5pm	Bladder
5pm – 7pm	Kidneys
7pm – 9pm	Circulatory System
9pm – 11pm	Triple Heater (Endocrine System)
11pm – 1am	Gall Bladder

The organs in the human body also get activated from the meridians at a certain time of day following a natural daily rhythm.

Whether we like it or not, our bodies follow an internal body clock. According to Traditional Chinese Medicine (and other ancient healing traditions in Asia), vital energy flows through the 12 organs, each organ has its points of highest energy and lowest energy, and every 24 hours a cycle is completed. The 'Traditional Chinese Organ Body Clock' on page 2 shows at what time of the day various organs are activated.

Francis Bacon (1561-1626), an English philosopher, statesman, scientist, jurist, orator, essayist, and author, once advised: "We can only master nature by complying to her laws."

To inhale or exhale, to be asleep or awake, to be stressed or relaxed are opposites which balance each other out in an ongoing rhythm.

Nowadays it can be a challenge for people to deliberately follow natural rhythms. To take hold or let go, to be active or passive... the right timing of these balancing movements defines a sustainable lifestyle. If we disrupt the rhythmical return of the opposites, we neglect a most important balance in our lives. Without the balancing of extremes, we get sick.

Many strive for permanence in a fast-paced lifestyle. Isn't there permanence in the rhythmic return of polarities? And doesn't this rhythm enrich our lives?

We cannot turn back the wheels of time, but there is always a choice and an innovative way to integrate nature's rhythms into our lives. Your interest in this book mirrors the intention of many – the pursuit of a more sustainable lifestyle.

Nature's Almanac "Nature's Daily Guide to Success" offers you successful guidelines to include the influence of the lunar cycle into living a better, healthier, and more successful life. Since 1997 this calendar has been a reliable guide and helper for many. This reference book offers an introduction into the lunar cycle and its effects on nature and our lives. Here you will find a collection of information on the subject collected from many different sources of mostly European origin[4]. If you are already familiar with Nature's Almanac, this book will enrich your insights into the lunar cycle. Improved knowledge of the lunar cycle's effects will ease their application in your daily life. Many activities have the greatest chance of success if they are in tune with nature's rhythms, saving you time, effort, and money while also guiding you to live a more efficient and sustainable way of life.

How to use a lunar calendar and almanac?

A lunar calendar and almanac serves you as a particularly useful tool for your daily activities. Applying the suggested best timing, your activities will be completed efficiently and successfully, helping you avoid hit-or-miss results and achieve sustained success. If you apply the rules for favorable and unfavorable activities, you can avoid damage, failure, stress, sickness, and discouragement.

For example, on certain days problem stains are removed more easily, and windows are cleaned without leaving streaks. Schedule your hair care for the most favorable days and your hair retains its form and beauty longer, hair dyes will look more vibrant, and frizzy hair can be avoided. If you incorporate the lunar cycle, you will improve and get the most benefit from body care and health treatments.

Considering the effect the moon has on certain body parts, you can maximize the results from medicines, supplements, and detox measures. Optimize your efforts while exercising certain body parts.

Plan your business meetings on days when people are most open for negotiating, networking, and exchanging ideas. Learn about the days when it's advisable to focus on financial matters or routine work.

Planning your meals based on the advice of the lunar calendar, you can optimize for the best health and well-being. Get the best growth from your plants, optimize your harvest, and take advantage of sustainable gardening methods when you garden according to the moon's rhythm.

These are only a few of the many ways you can apply the influence of the lunar cycle to improve your life. Even skeptics become convinced by the actual results. More and more people are incorporating nature's rhythms into their daily lives.

The Nature's Almanac identifies the moon's phases and the exact times the moon travels through the sections of the lunar cycle. You don't have to memorize symbols and their meanings; this lunar calendar lists daily everything that is most beneficial for yielding the best outcomes as well as anything that's unfavorable to do and would result in adverse outcomes.

For ease of use of the lunar calendar, everything is organized into the columns of success, leisure time, health, body care, garden/nature, housework, and nutrition. You will quickly gain a general overview of each day. To plan ahead just consider the advice in the columns and mark what's important to you. Each page offers plenty of space to add your notes in the agenda section.

I hope the reader will gain insights from this book that may be a constant source of information and inspiration to live in harmony with nature.

Edith Stadig

1. An Introduction to the Lunar Cycle

"There is no chance in life, only harmony and order."
Plotin, Greek Philosopher

The moon has been known since prehistoric times. It is not just an object of research in science but also appears in the arts, literature, myths, legends, and poetry. In some nature and pagan religions the moon was worshiped as a deity and plays a part in magic traditions. Music and arts praised its magic and beauty. From 1961 to 1969 the USSR and the United States were locked in a history-making race to land the first human on the moon.

The moon has an influence on the history of mankind, the lives of great leaders as well as everyday men and women. It has an effect on all of nature and our well-being, even on our daily activities in multiple areas of life.

The lunar cycle is based on scientific findings and astronomical data. For centuries our ancestors observed the effects of the lunar cycle. Now science is gradually catching up on an influence so subtle and intricate but nevertheless key to a life in harmony with nature.

1.1. The Findings of Science

The Lunar Cycle

The moon is the earth's only natural satellite and after the sun the second brightest object in the sky. It makes a complete orbit around the earth in approximately 29.5 days. The angle between the earth, moon, and sun changes during the moon's elliptical orbit. We see this as the cycle of the moon's phases. Every 29.5 days, the New Moon transits through its waxing phase into the Full Moon and during its waning phase into the next New Moon.

Fig. 1.a:
It takes 29.5 days for the moon to orbit around the earth. (Dimensions are not proportional.)

The Rotation of the Earth

Earth completes a rotation around its own axis every 24 hours. Because of the earth's rotation, the moon seems to rotate once a day around the earth when viewed from the earth. We see the moon every day rising and setting. Depending on the moon's position during its 29.5-day elliptical orbit around the earth, we see the crescent, the New Moon, or the Full Moon. Due to the tidal effects of the moon, the earth's rotation is slowing slightly with time. A modern day is about 1.7 milliseconds longer than it was a century ago.

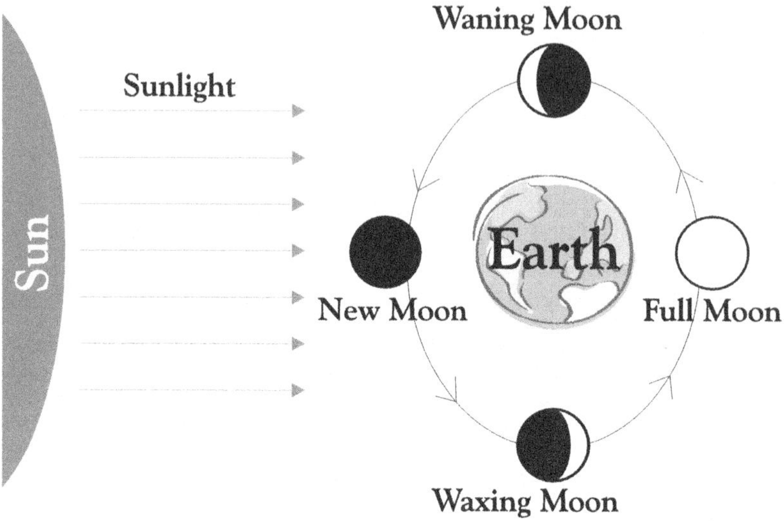

Fig. 1.b:
Depending on the moon's position during its elliptical orbit around the earth, we see the crescent, the New Moon, or the Full Moon from the earth. (Dimensions are not proportional.)

The Tides

The gravitational forces between the earth and the moon cause some interesting effects, the most obvious being the tides. Since the earth rotates around its own axis, each day every spot on the earth comes close to the moon and then moves away again. Because of the gravitational forces, the changing distance from the moon makes a difference on the earth's surface and causes the tides. This effect is much stronger in the ocean than in the solid crust. The ocean bulges and high tide occurs.

But why do we experience two high tides over the course of a day, once with the moon in its zenith and again nearly 12 hours later? Besides the gravitational pull there is also a force which pulls the ocean layer away from the moon, not unlike what happens to the water in a pail when you swing it in a circle. On the near side of the moon the direct pull dominates and causes the oceans to bulge toward the moon, while on the far side the centrifugal effect dominates and causes the oceans to bulge away from the moon. Any given seaside location will experience a high tide when the moon is at its closest, and then another one about 12 hours later when it is at its furthest.

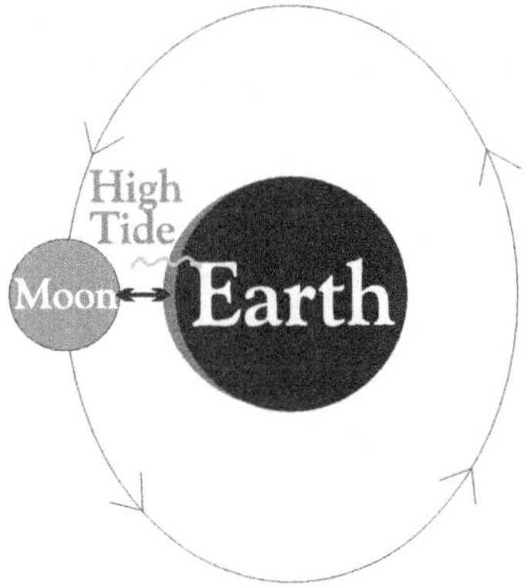

Fig. 1.c:
During its orbit around the earth the moon effects a gravitational pull on the earth's surface, causing high tides in the areas of the ocean closest to the moon. (Dimensions are not proportional.)

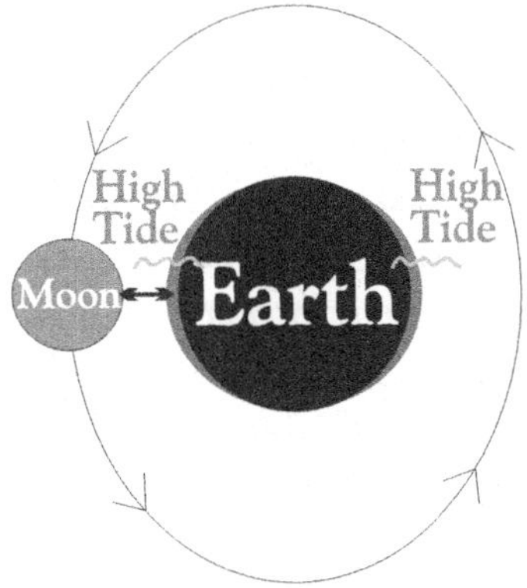

Fig. 1.d:
A gravitational pull from the moon and a centrifugal effect cause simultaneous high tides on opposite sides of the earth. (Dimensions are not proportional.)

The gravitational forces between the earth and the moon are not limited to the effects on the oceans. They also have an impact on water in the earth crust and in all living things, plants, animals, and humans. Only the tides are visible to the naked eye.

During the orbit of the moon the distance between the earth and the moon varies. The closest distance at the perigee is 225,622 miles. The farthest distance at the apogee is 252,088 miles.

1.2. The Findings of Astrology

Ancient cultures of the Mediterranean and the Middle East studied the night sky and named each group of stars, specifying the zodiac and the zodiac signs. The mapping of the zodiac signs describe symbolically and pictorially the characteristic attributes of the zodiac signs and their forces. For example, the characteristics of the zodiac sign of Aries assembles those of a young, untamed ram running zestfully over spring meadows, ready to ram down obstacles with its horns... Indeed in astrology Aries' impact is described as energetic, aggressive, enthusiastic, and heady. Every zodiac sign is described in detail in chapter 2.

Dividing the year into 12 sections, astrology designates 12 different zodiac signs. Each sign matches a certain group or cluster of stars. Unlike the Gregorian calendar, the astrological year does not start on January 1st but with the spring equinox on March 21st. The cluster of stars the sun travels through from March 21st through April 20th is named Aries. Subsequent star clusters or groups are Taurus, Gemini, Cancer, Leo, Virgo, Libra, Scorpio, Sagittarius, Capricorn, Aquarius, concluding with Pisces.

Your star sign is appointed by the zodiac sign in which the sun traveled at the time of your birth. If you are born for example between March 21st and April 20th, your star sign is Aries.

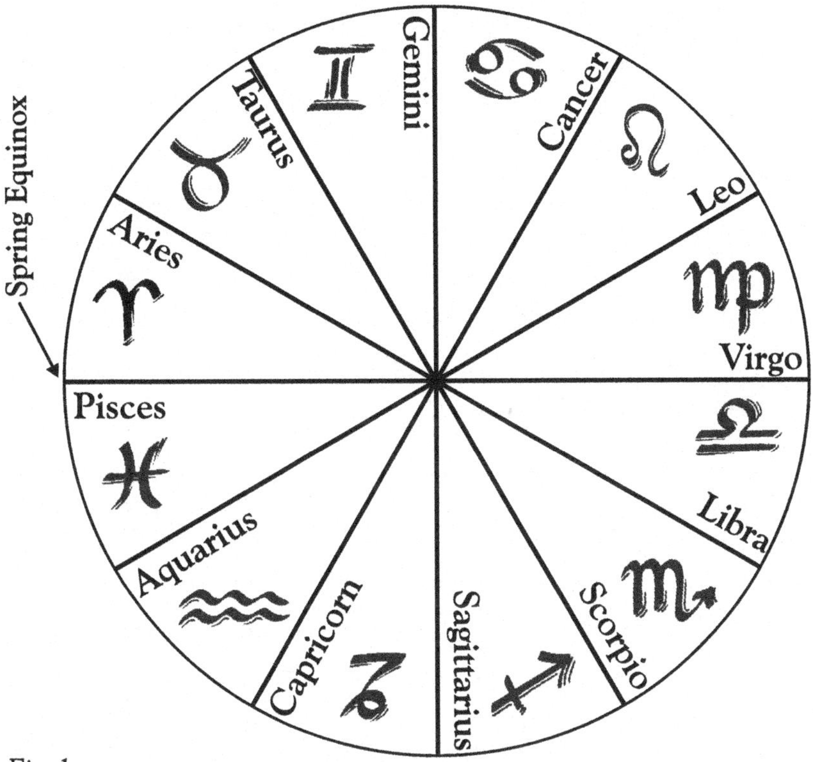

Fig. 1.e:
The zodiac consists of 12 sections, the zodiac signs.

Even though the section of each zodiac sign on the chart has the same size, in reality they have slightly different sizes. This is due to the elliptical orbit of the earth around the sun and the rounding of the orbits to full days. Hence the zodiac sign of Capricorn lasts only 29 days, while the zodiac sign Leo lasts 31 days.

Just like the sun, the moon also travels through all of the zodiac signs. But while the sun takes 356 days to travel through all zodiac signs and 29 to 31 days to travel through a single sign, the moon only takes 28 days for all zodiac signs and hence stays only 2 to 3 day in a single sign.

A regular daily calendar page is sectioned off based on the earth's rotation around its axis and the resulting phases of days and nights.

A lunar calendar, however, is based on the duration the moon takes to travel through the zodiac signs. Since it takes the moon 2 to 3 days to travel through one zodiac sign, many lunar calendars are divided into one page or one section for every 2 to 3 days.

The zodiac sign the moon travels through on any given day as well as the layout of a lunar calendar do NOT correlate to the star sign of any person, since the star sign is determined by the zodiac sign the sun is positioned in at the time of one's birth.

The page layout in a lunar calendar is based on the moon traveling through a zodiac sign.

The exact time the moon transitions from one zodiac sign into the next is listed in the ephemeris, an annual publication giving the positions of the sun, moon, and planets during the course of a year, information concerning eclipses, astronomical constants, etc. However, most lunar calendars do not list the exact time of transition.

1.3. What Our Ancestors Observed

Indigenous people always lived in close connection with nature's rhythms. The natural world was central to their economic, spiritual, physical, and cultural well-being. For centuries they observed the effects and results of their activities in connection with nature's rhythms. They measured and compared their observations, including the movements and constellations of celestial bodies and the lunar cycle, the latter being readily observable both in rhythm and appearance. It was easy for them to track the moon and its phases as well as its position in the night sky and in relation to other groups of stars.

Indigenous people did not have the knowledge of gravitational forces as modern science teaches. But patient observation made them aware of the lunar influence on nature, plants, animals, and humans. They discovered how to utilize the influence of the lunar cycle to improve the harvest, the health of plants, animals, and humans, forestry, building, crafting, cooking, and preserving as well as to explain psychological fluctuations and human interrelations. The positive outcome of their activities was often crucial to survival. The observations made reliable forecasts possible, thereby providing a valuable transfer of knowledge to future generations.

1.4. ● New Moon – A New Beginning

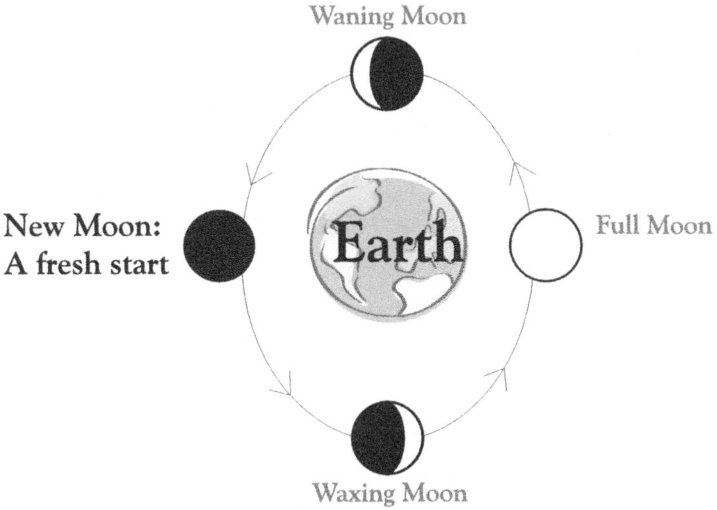

Fig. 1.f: The New Moon symbolizes a new beginning.

- The body detoxifies most efficiently.
- Self-healing powers peak.
- Ingestion of food slows down.
- Day of fasting helps to prevent illnesses and promote health.
- Dropping bad habits is easier.
- Make decisions and confirm your resolutions.
- Care for sickly plants.
- Change of weather is likely.

New Moon is the end point of waning moon and at the same time the beginning of a new cycle. As the closure of the preceding waning moon phase, New Moon is the culmination of the body's abilities to detoxify and its powers of self-healing. However, even though the healing powers are at a peak, any kind of surgery is to be avoided if possible.

On New Moon the body detoxifies most efficiently, but ingestion of food likely slows down. A day of fasting on a New Moon day promotes health and can prevent illnesses.

This is also the best day to drop bad habits, change directions if necessary, confirm your resolutions, and finalize new decisions. Body and mind are more likely to stay calm and balanced in the face of changes, withdrawal, or loss.

The care of sickly plants is most effective during New Moon. Weather changes and short-term climate changes are to be anticipated.

1.5. ☽ **Waxing Moon** – The Inhale

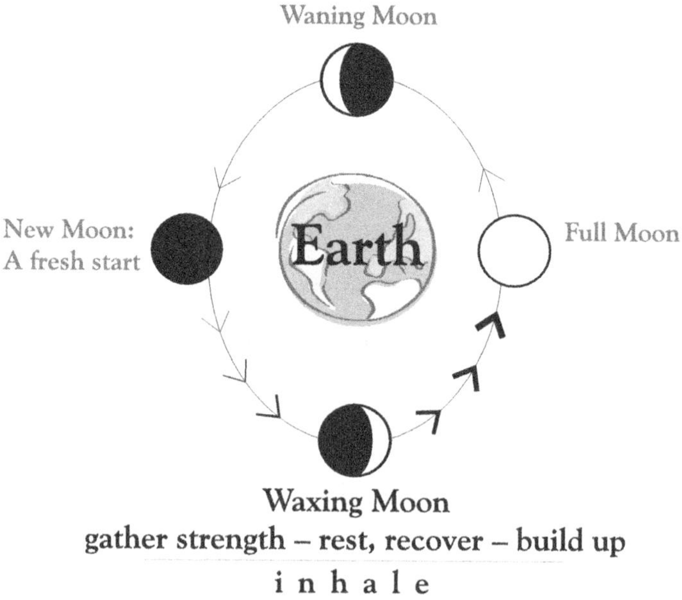

Fig 1.g: Waxing moon – the inhale.

- Gather strength, rest, and recover.
- The body absorbs more readily.
- Weight gain is easier.
- Supply nutrient materials to strengthen the body.
- Stimulants and vitamins have a stronger effect.
- The closer it is to Full Moon, the stronger the waxing moon phase's impact will be.

For the duration of about two weeks while the moon is waxing, nature transitions through the first half of the moon cycle. Following the active phase during the waning moon, now it's time to rest, recover, and regroup. This section of the lunar cycle can be described as the inhale of nature, a time to rest in order to collect and regain strength.

Since the body readily absorbs during this time, you are more likely to gain weight even with regular amount of food intake. Therefore avoid indulging in rich foods. If you are overweight, eat smaller portions.

Everything that is supplied to build up and strengthen the body is most effective. Stimulants and vitamins have a stronger effect. The closer it is to Full Moon, the stronger the waxing moon phase's impact will be.

Now is the perfect time to plan ahead and restructure. Go easy and take time to relax with the goal of gathering strength for the active phase of the waning moon. Most likely you feel less energetic as during the waning moon phase. Slow down, take it easy, and trust in nature's rhythm. If you get plenty of rest during the waxing moon phase, nature will provide you with renewed energies for the waning moon phase.

Any deficiencies of minerals and/or vitamins in the body are best taken care of during the waxing moon. Include all important supplements, tonics, and herbs in your diet. Focus on foods that contain essential minerals and vitamins your body is lacking.

Drugs have a much stronger effect. All measures taken to supply nutrient materials and strengthen the sensitive body parts are very effective. Be aware that the body also more readily absorbs poisonous substances. The body retains water more easily, and diuretic measures don't work as effectively. Any healing ointments are easily absorbed.

The closer it is to Full Moon, the better it is to stay away from any surgery if possible, because healing and recovery will take longer and scarring will be more severe.

Execute all flexible measures to relax, restore, strengthen, and build up more effectively during the waxing moon phase.

1.6. ○ Full Moon – The Break

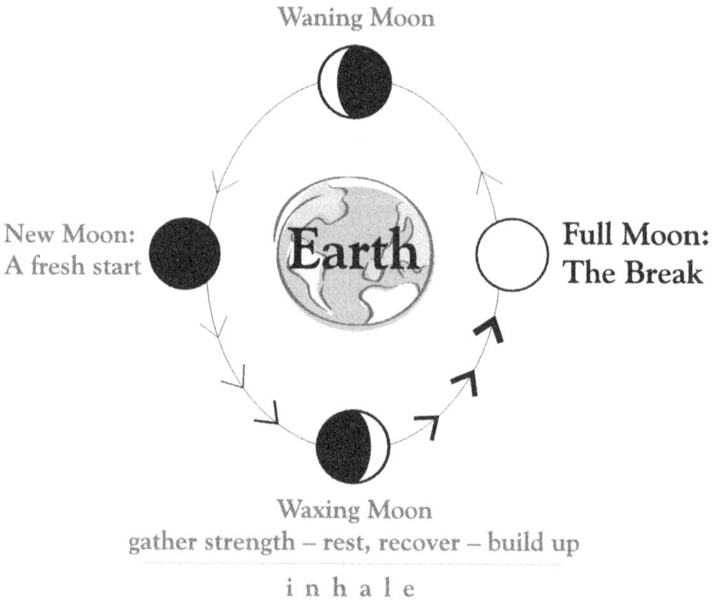

Fig. 1.h: The Full Moon symbolizes the break and turning point of the lunar cycle.

- The body utilizes nutrition most effectively.
- Avoid artificial flavors and additives.
- Day of fasting helps to prevent illnesses and promote health.
- Wounds might bleed more.
- Avoid surgery and vaccination.
- Healing herbs collected on Full Moon are more powerful.
- Change of weather is likely.

At Full Moon, nature's inhale during the waxing moon comes to a standstill, culminating in a break and the turning point of the cycle. This means "the calm before the storm," the calm before the phase of activity of the waning moon phase.

A day of fasting on a Full Moon day promotes health and can prevent illnesses. Be cautious and aware since the body utilizes nutrition most effectively during this time, it acts the same on any artificial flavors, additives, stimulants, drugs as well as poisonous substances.

Wounds might bleed more profusely than other times. Recovery after surgery is impeded. Vaccinations are unfavorable in the three days before and on Full Moon. The body is more likely to retain water. Healing herbs collected on Full Moon have greater curative power. Like on New Moon days, weather changes and short-term climate changes are to be anticipated.

1.7. ☾ Waning Moon – The Exhale

For the duration of about two weeks, while the moon is waning, nature transitions through the second half of the moon cycle. After the phase of rest during waxing moon, now it's time to be active, detoxify, and remove. This cycle section can be described as the exhale of nature.

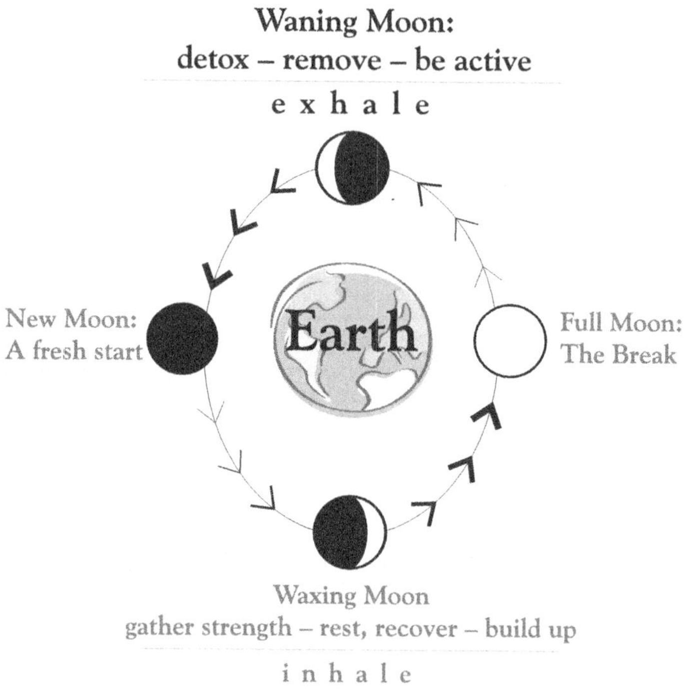

Fig. 1.i: Waning Moon – the exhale.

- Detoxify, remove, and be active.
- Detoxing and cleansing processes are advised.
- Weight gain is less likely.
- Surgical operations and dental treatments tend to be more successful.
- Housework yields better results.
- The closer it is to New Moon, the stronger the waning moon phase's impact will be.

The body is ready to detoxify and cleanse, and weight gain associated with overeating is less likely. Anybody underweight should consider eating larger portions.

All measures taken to flush out and detoxify the sensitive body parts are very effective. The closer to New Moon the stronger the

impact of the forces and effects of the waning moon phase. During the waning moon any cleansing and detox diets will yield the best results. Herbal teas, steam room, sauna... anything to detoxify and cleanse are best utilized between Full Moon and New Moon.

The body tends to heal faster during the waning moon and the success rates of surgeries are much higher. If you have the choice, schedule operations accordingly. Scarring is less severe, wounds most likely will bleed less during the waning moon, and surgical operations in general are less taxing on the body. To yield the best results, schedule dental treatments at this time, such as removal of tartar and amalgam as well as fillings, crowns, and dentures.

But the positive effect of cleansing extends beyond our bodies into the environment as well. Dirt and pollution are best dealt with during the waning moon. House cleaning, car washing, laundry... dirt and spots are removed more easily, and cleaning agents are more efficient.

The waning moon phase asks us to be active and apply all our energies at activities around the house, at work and at school, in the garden, at sports or other leisure activities. You reach your goals more easily and yield better results compared to the waxing moon phase.

Execute all flexible measures to detoxify and cleanse effectively during the waning moon.

1.8. The Transition

The moon's exact transition time from one zodiac sign into the next is listed in the ephemeris. Only a few lunar calendars list the exact time of transition. Some lunar calendars list the daily zodiac sign not according to the exact time of transition but according to the zodiac sign the moon is in at midnight.

With the exact time listed you know exactly what quality is dominant throughout any given day. If the transition occurs after noon, the dominant quality of the day is given by the previous zodiac sign. Any transition before noon suggests the qualities of the new zodiac sign ruling the day.

Rather than precisely to the minute, the transition is a gradual change and overlapping of the forces. For critical decisions you may consider the time of transition.

Some people sense the transition into the next zodiac sign. Most noticeable is the transition from Pisces into Aries which at times can be felt as pressure on or in the head.

1.9. Half Moon

Half Moon marks the midpoint between Full Moon and New Moon during waxing as well as waning moon phases. After approximately seven days of each waxing moon and waning moon, the Half Moon is reached.

2. Introduction to the Effects of the Zodiac Signs

"Know, that you are a little world of your own
And the sun and moon are within you
As well as the stars."
Origen Adamantius

Astrology divides the year into 12 sections starting at the spring equinox, the First Point of Aries. Called zodiac signs, these parts each match a certain cluster of stars. Aries is the name of the star cluster the sun travels through from March 21st through April 20th. Subsequently following Aries are the star clusters or groups of Taurus, Gemini, Cancer, Leo, Virgo, Libra, Scorpio, Sagittarius, Capricorn, Aquarius, concluding with Pisces.

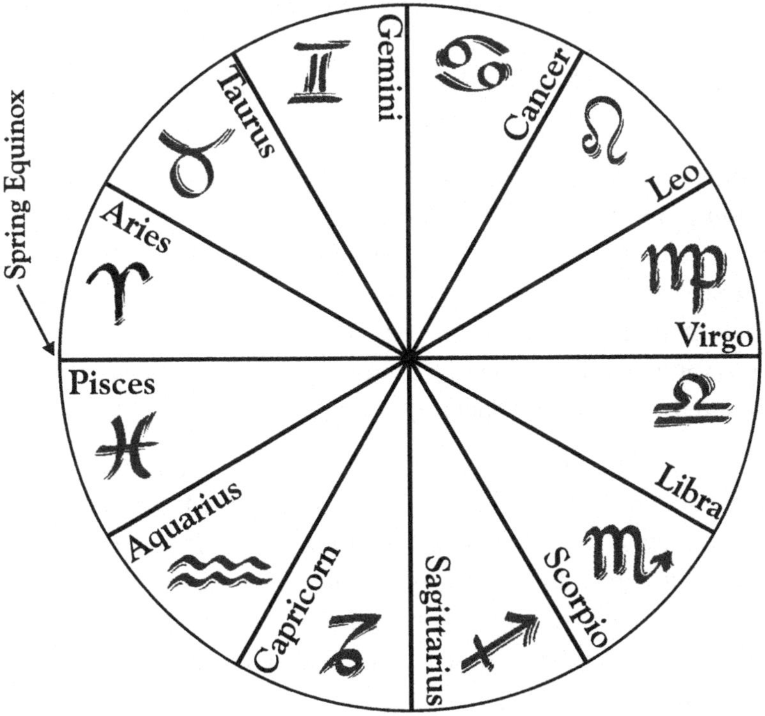

Fig. 2.a: The zodiac consists of 12 sections of the zodiac signs.

The zodiac chart depicts all zodiac signs in the order the sun travels through them during the course of a year and the moon during the duration of two to three days.

Astrology assigned a specific symbol to each zodiac sign/star cluster. The designation of the zodiac signs didn't happen randomly; they describe symbolically and pictorially the characteristic attributes of the zodiac signs and their forces.

As mentioned before in section 1.2., even though the section of each zodiac sign on the chart has the same size, in reality they have slightly different sizes. The reason for this is the elliptical orbit of the earth around the sun and the rounding of the orbits to full days. Hence the zodiac sign of Capricorn lasts only 29 days, while the zodiac sign Leo lasts 31 days.

Similar to the sun, the moon also travels through all of the zodiac signs. The sun takes 356 days to travel through all zodiac signs and 29 to 31 days to travel through each single sign, while the moon only takes 28 days for all zodiac signs and 2 to 3 days for each single sign.

A standard daily calendar is sectioned off according to the earth's rotation around its axis and the resulting phases of day and night. A lunar calendar is based on the time the moon travels through a zodiac sign. Because it takes the moon 2 to 3 days to travel through a zodiac sign, many lunar calendars are divided in one page or one section for every 2 to 3 days, meaning one page or one section for each sign the moon is journeying through.

This rhythm of pages or section of 2 to 3 days per zodiac sign is interspersed at times by the Full Moon and New Moon. If the Full Moon or New Moon occurs at the middle of a zodiac sign section, then this sign gets divided into a waxing and a waning phase. It may result for example in a page with 1 day of waxing moon of a specific zodiac sign and then 1 or 2 days of waning moon of the same zodiac sign.

2.1. Descriptions of the Zodiac Signs

Each zodiac sign displays many different facets, and the following descriptions will allow deeper insight into the characteristic traits of each sign. Some of the characteristics you might recognize in people you know. However, keep in mind that the personality traits of each person are not limited to the sun sign, but are influenced by the positions of other planets and their constellations in the birth horoscope as well as by current positions and constellations. In addition it is important to consider that the way people express themselves varies by different levels of personal development and stages in life.

Reading through the descriptions of the zodiac signs will give you an overview into each sign, enabling you to better understand their respective influence and effect on the quality of any given day as described in the lunar calendar. It will be easy to comprehend, for example, why on days when the moon travels in Cancer you may feel like retreating into the coziness of your home instead of mingling with people at a party.

Aries

__Strengths:__

Determination, drive, enthusiasm, courage, willpower, spontaneity, initiative, self-confidence, zeal, and enterprising spirit.

__Weeknesses:__

Impatience, headiness, single-mindedness, quick temper, recklessness, and selfishness.

The astrological symbol of Aries pictures a force which starts from one point spreading out like a fountain. It depicts also the horns of a ram, indicating the ram is ready for combat.

The new beginning starts at spring equinox. Aries resembles a young, untamed ram running zestfully over spring meadows, ready to ram obstacles with its horns. In astrology Aries' traits are described as energetic, aggressive, enthusiastic, and heady.

Aries is also spontaneous and courageous, and for its own ideas and interests the force can move "head first through a wall," exhibiting impatience and willingness to take risks. Aries acts with a natural self-confidence.

But with its quick temper Aries often makes decisions thoughtlessly and too quickly. A solitary fighter it does not find it easy to work well in a team. Although the Aries force can be helpful, straight, and honest, it still prefers to follow its own way and dislikes being told what to do.

Taurus

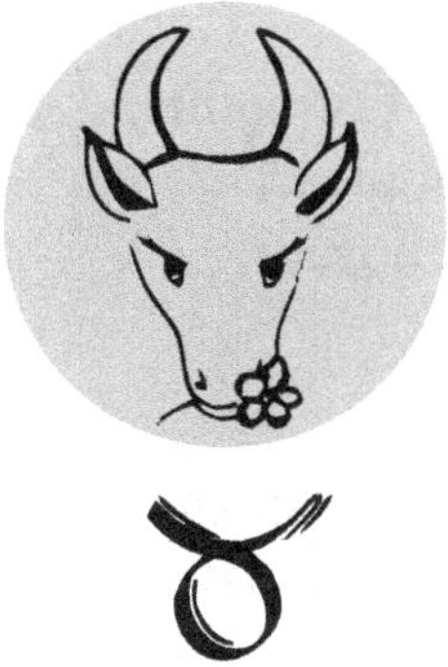

Strengths:
Security, perseverance, loyalty, grounded in reality, levelheadedness, peacefulness, order, assertiveness, vitality, benevolence, and diligence.

Weeknesses:
Stubbornness, waywardness, vengefulness, intemperateness, and taciturnity.

The symbol of Taurus is pictured as a bowl and circle. The bowl collects, for people with strong Taurus traits most likely easily accumulate material property, and they also like to indulge in tasty foods. The bowl symbolizes softness, gentleness, a leisurely pace, and a preference for comfort. The closed circle represents taciturnity, as Taurus tends to be quiet, reserved, and safeguarding.

A peaceful bull grazing leisurely in the lush meadow, step by step he discovers his environment. He meets change deliberately and considers carefully. He is reliable and levelheaded, with a preference for pleasure. Practical-minded, he rarely loses the ground underneath his feet.

A Taurus person likes to socialize and pamper guests, striving for stability and beauty. The latter is important not only for looks but also for surroundings.

Being somewhat slow, Taurus people at times submit too readily to idleness or sluggishness. Rarely are they in a bad mood, but if so, it lasts for a long time, feeding resentments and vengefulness. Like peaceful cattle turning into raging bulls, temper tantrums are infrequent but can turn very fierce if Taurus personalities become aggravated.

Gemini

Strengths:
Communications, flexibility, agility, articulateness, wealth of ideas, sociability, friendliness, humor, and studiousness.

Weeknesses:
Absent-mindedness, carelessness, nosiness, restlessness, garrulousness, and spirit of contradiction.

The astrological sign of Gemini pictures two vertical lines, symbolizing the proverbial two faces as well as the versatility of Gemini, who easily manages multitasking. The bowl on top stands for qualities of receiving like inquisitiveness and the thirst for knowledge. The bottom bowl represents the ability to yield, to pass on information.

Gemini are twins, two persons centered around communication. Gemini has a zest for learning and self-reflects by looking into the mirror at its twin. People with typical Gemini traits enjoy small talk, but their incessant stream of information often lacks depth. They react quickly on any impulse, and enjoy intellectual stimulation. This trait, however, can lead to restlessness, nervousness, and garrulousness.

The Gemini force easily absorbs new fields of knowledge and reacts with versatility in many different situations, enjoys traveling and new acquaintances. But with lack of stimulation Gemini quickly gets bored and loses interest.

Cancer

Strengths:
Empathy, solicitousness, receptiveness, insight, domesticity, emotionalism, tactfulness, protection, and affection.

Weeknesses:
Suggestibility, moodiness, irreconcilability, crankiness, and imperiousness.

In the astrological sign of Cancer two closed circles symbolizing spirit and creation are enwrapped in two bowls. The bowls are opened toward each other to form a protective cocoon around the two circles like a crab shell.

A crab has a hard shell and a soft core, and it moves sideways instead of forward. To save itself from danger it digs itself deep down into the sand. Typical Cancer personalities' out and forward movements alternate with retreats into the security of home. With ample imagination they perceive their surrounding mostly through their feelings.

The Cancer personality enjoys a comfortable and cozy home with home and family life being most important. Cancer types frequently tend to smother and hover over their dear ones. But the devotion they offer to others they also expect to receive in return, or else they turn moody and frustrated.

Being sensitive, receptive, and emotional, Cancer types turn moody quickly and don't handle a hectic pace and stress very well. Their surroundings are meaningful to them and are supposed to inspire and support their dreamworld.

Leo

Strengths:
Courage, talent to organize, generosity, zest for life, purpose, creative power, self-confidence, dauntlessness, and charisma.

Weeknesses:
Pride, arrogance, egocentricity, imperiousness, vanity, self-indulgence, bragging, and impulsiveness.

Whereas the circle, as symbol of creation, is protected by a bowl in the Cancer sign, in the sign of Leo it is stretched out, allowing the inner power to radiate outward. The arch in the sign points to the charisma of Leo. The circle is also a symbol of the sun, its ecliptic represented by the arch.

Leo, as the lion, is the king of all animals. Proud and with an aristocratic bearing, it is positioned on the top rung. Leo as the party animal likes to take center stage, and with their sweeping charm, much-admired, Leo types gift their audience with generosity and benevolence.

Their strength is self-confidence yet their weakness is shallowness. Their pomposity tolerates no criticism. When they feel they are being ignored they answer with explosive outbursts. They appoint their companions to enhance their prestige, and deep sympathy is not their talent.

Virgo

♍

Strengths:
Orderliness, diligence, reason, calmness, readiness to help, perfectionism, classification, skillfulness, and critical faculty.

Weeknesses:
Pedantry, censoriousness, discontentment, nagging, and materialism.

Three upside down bowls and an arch pointing to the left make up the astrological symbol of Virgo. Everything is collected and stockpiled under the bowls, ordered and protected, displaying frugality and the preference to hide from public view. The stockpiling also indicates wisdom. Furthermore the sign depicts the focus on the inner worlds of Virgo.

After the excesses of party life during Leo reign it's time to get life back in order. Virgo steps in with diligence and steadiness, assuming responsibility. With practical mindedness Virgo people absorb what goes on around them and with analytical thinking pass judgment.

In the western hemisphere the sun travels through Virgo during harvest time. Virgo is intimately connected to nature and plants. Natural shyness prevents new connections from being dictated by passion instead they are rather carefully planned. Orderliness may lead to pedantry, and disappointments can easily lead Virgo into nagging, resignation, and bitterness.

Libra

<u>Strengths:</u>
Diplomacy, sense of justice, pursuit of harmony, aesthetics, open-mindedness, politeness, frankness, helpfulness, judiciousness, and conviviality.

<u>Weeknesses:</u>
Fickleness, indulgence in comfort, unsteadiness, indecisiveness, and indifference.

The astrological sign of Libra symbolizes the sun setting on the horizon. The two horizontal lines stand for joint paths. Libra is the conciliator, remaining unswayed between extremes, pursuing and establishing balance and harmony.

Following busy and diligent Virgo, Libra contributes with love for beauty and art. While striving for harmony, Libra is sociable and willing to compromise.

Libra always looks at both sides of the coin and carefully deliberates. Habitually going back and forth between their own interest and others, Libra types always strive for balance. Able to see both sides Libra has a good sense of justice, but this can also result in indecisiveness or going back and forth, which others will perceive as fickleness and unsteadiness.

Scorpio

Strengths:
Assertiveness, tirelessness, endurance, diligence, determination, insight-fullness, profundity, loyalty, idealism, instinct, and passion.

Weeknesses:
Distrust, fanaticism, unwillingness to compromise, taciturnity, vindictiveness, and vulnerability to lower instincts.

Similar to the Virgo sign, the astrological sign of Scorpio also shows three upside down bowls hiding content from public view. This symbolizes Scorpio's taciturnity, profundity, and secretiveness. The arrow reminds of a lethal poisoned arrow like the sting of a deadly scorpion. Pointing outward, the arrow represents the possibility of explosions of energies.

Scorpio is occupied if not possessed with the shallows, abyss, and depths of humanity. Sexuality, suffering, and death are of interest. Conflicts don't get avoided, and the poisonous sting can be lethal to any attacker.

Attachment to passion and addiction to problems can make life difficult for a Scorpio person and people around him. Guided by instincts, Scorpio displays endurance and assertiveness. Aggressiveness can quickly turn cynical, bossy, and self-opinionated.

Sagittarius

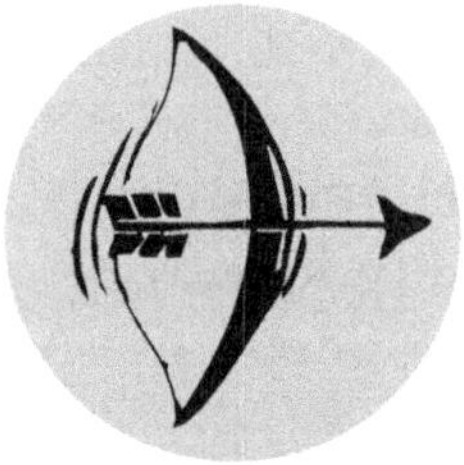

Strengths:
Persuasive power, enthusiasm, optimism, desire for unlimited freedom, enterprising spirit, zest for adventure, charity, sportsmanship, open-heartedness, openness to new experiences.

Weeknesses:
Rashness, bragging, meddling, imposture, restlessness, stubbornness, and ambivalence.

The astrological sign of Sagittarius pictures an arrow pointing to the right and outward, signifying an impulsive forward move and change of direction. The arrow points toward a distant shore, and people with Sagittarius traits love to travel and explore the vastness of nature. The cross depicted in the sign represents insight and a strong connection to the earth.

With bow and arrow the archer Sagittarius aims for new experiences and insights. Every change, every progress has its goal. Open to diversity, change, mobility, and travel, Sagittarius always looks for expansion and freedom.

With the talent of a good teacher, Sagittarius types like to inspire others. A sense of justice and respect for their fellow beings govern their thinking. Unfortunately in their love of adventure they overestimate their strength. They can turn into showoffs and are often unable to admit fault.

Capricorn

Strengths:
Perseverance, discipline, responsibility, ambition, endurance, patience, practicality, soberness, thoroughness, willpower, and seriousness.

Weeknesses:
Obstinacy, frigidity, compulsion, pessimism, stubbornness, and hardheartedness.

The arch symbolizing the roof of the world is anchored by a main pillar in the astrological sign of Capricorn. The closed circle reveals steadfastness for its content, and a root-like extension reaches deep into the ground.

Capricorn is comparable to an ibex living in meager, desolate mountain regions under hard conditions for survival. An ibex can survive in barren regions, for no rock is too steep to climb. Frugal and disciplined, practical Capricorn is ready for any possible outcome. Unspoiled from any affluence, Capricorn wisely uses resources and acts responsibly.

Defending themselves with their horns, Capricorns can be stubborn, holding on blindly to old convictions. Steeped in dull pessimism, life can turn laborious and lead to depression.

Aquarius

Strengths:
Originality, imagination, visions, individuality, independence, idealism, agility, inventiveness, responsiveness, and progressiveness.

Weeknesses:
Rebelliousness, aloofness, unpredictability, and selfishness.

In the astrological sign of Aquarius, two waves on top of each other symbolize power, currents, and electricity. Power in all its different facets, as alternating current as well as the impulses running through the nerves. Both waves flow toward the right side, representing the open-minded and future-oriented sight of Aquarius.

Aquarius dwells remotely high above in his ivory tower reading visions of a better future in the stars. He glances down, belittling humanity from afar. To express his originality and his idealism, independence is quintessential for Aquarius, who is always on the move. The imagination and inventiveness of Aquarius spread to many different areas of life. As a rebel or reformer, Aquarius breaks open the solidified formations of Capricorn.

People with Aquarius traits can be entertaining yet unpredictable and unreliable, often unable to transform their promises into actions. Feeling drawn toward anything new, they shy away from routine tasks.

Pisces

Strengths:

Intuition, readiness to help others, empathy, sensibility, imagination, tactfulness, peacefulness, desire for transcendence and expansion of consciousness.

Weeknesses:

Fickleness, hypersensitivity, instability, suggestibility, and tendency to withdrawal.

In this astrological sign, the dual soul of Pisces is pictured in two bowls turned against and closed to each other. One side doesn't know what the other is up to, which is a hint to the inner riddle, the mystery as well as a certain fickleness of Pisces. Additionally the Pisces sign pictures the waxing and waning moon. The horizontal line connects and represents a timeline dismantling the old before building up the new.

The circle of the zodiac is completed with the sign of Pisces symbolizing the closure of this world, transcendence, and the crossing over to the beyond. Pisces are drawn to magic and mystic. They offer compassion and attend to minorities and outcasts, not shying away from the dark side of life. Possessing empathy, Pisces knows about the suffering of others and never offers help condescendingly.

Easy to persuade, Pisces finds it hard to set healthy boundaries but instead withdraws and dwells in the role of the victim to manipulate and get desires and wants fulfilled.

2.2. The Elements: Fire, Earth, Air, and Water

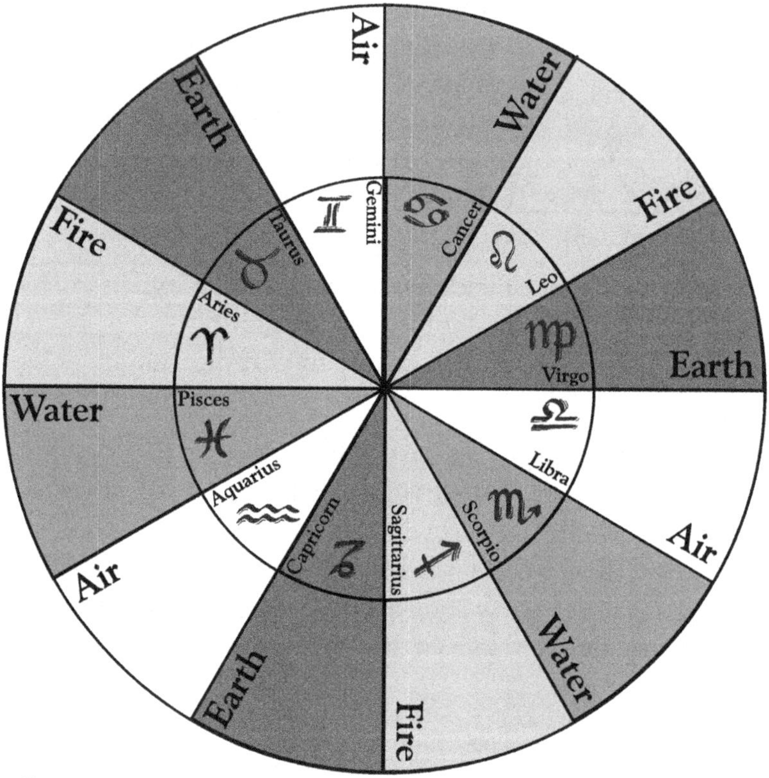

Fig. 2.a
Correlation of the elements fire, earth, air, and water with the zodiac signs.

Each zodiac sign correlates with one of the elements of fire, earth, air, and water. Each element brings its correspondent characteristics to the sign it is associated with.

Aries as the first sign in the zodiac represents the element of fire, Taurus is connected with the earth element, Gemini with the air element, and Cancer with the water element. Continuing through the zodiac, the sign of Leo represents the element of fire again, Virgo is connected with the earth element, and so on. The connections are not random but represent explicit characteristics of the respective zodiac signs.

Fire– Energy – "I will"

Aries, Leo, and Sagittarius all display energetic and fiery qualities representing the element of fire. In Aries these qualities are expressed in a rather inexperienced, heady, and premature way, while Sagittarius knows how to use them in more mature and experienced ways.

Earth – Methodology – "I act"

Taurus, Virgo, and Capricorn express well grounded characteristics connected to the element of earth. With patience, methodology, and perseverance they work toward their goals. Taurus prefers earthly pleasures, and Virgo displays healing, nurturing, and protective abilities. Capricorn can be resourceful and disciplined enough to survive in the most meager circumstances.

Air – Thoughts – "I think"

The element of air correlates to Gemini, Libra, and Aquarius. Indeed, they display a kind of airiness, observed as flexibility and mobility in thinking, acting, and feeling. Gemini is very talented in communication, and Libra is flexible and acknowledges coexisting vantage points. Aquarius displays flexibility in the fields of imagination and vision.

Water– Feelings – "I feel"

Water represents feelings and correlates with the signs of Cancer, Scorpio, and Pisces. The characteristics of water signs are sensibility and empathy. Cancer expresses these traits best in the areas of home and family, while Scorpio explores intensely and deeply the thresholds and marginal realms of feeling. Pisces uses intuition, sensitivity, and receptivity in feelings, striving to reach toward fathomless depths.

2.3. Qualities of the Day: Warm, Cool, Air/Light, and Wetness

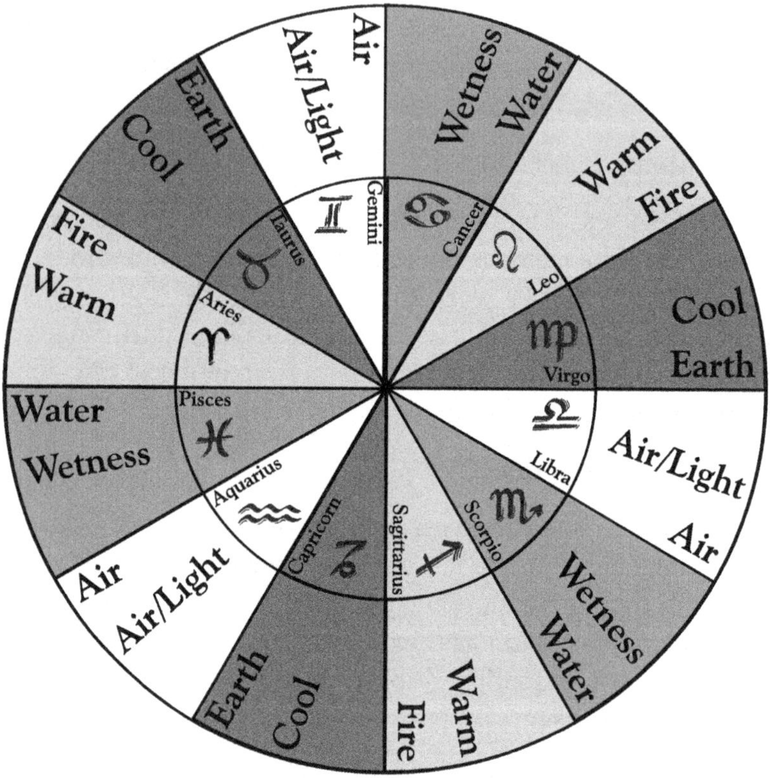

Fig. 2.b
The qualities of the day are linked with the elements: Warm, Cool, Air/Light, or Wetness.

Linked to the elements of fire, earth, air, and water, every day reveals a different quality. If the moon is traveling through the signs of Aries, Leo, or Sagittarius on any given day, the element of fire links this day with the quality of **WARM**. For the signs of Taurus, Virgo, and Capricorn the element of earth links to the quality of **COOL**, for Gemini, Libra, and Aquarius the element of air links to the quality of **AIR/LIGHT**, and for Cancer, Scorpio, and Pisces the element of water links to the quality of **WETNESS**.

The qualities can be felt on any given day. On a day with the quality of **WARM** for example, you sweat, dehydrate and get thirsty easily. Whereas if the quality of the day is **COOL**, you get chilly and may want to wear warmer clothing if you stay outside.

On days qualified as **AIR/LIGHT**, plants are capable of absorbing more light than other days. People sensitive to light might want to wear sunglasses even with overcast skies because the light feels pungent to the eyes.

With the quality of **WETNESS**, these respective days are unfavorable for any kind of painting task, since the paint takes much longer to dry. Plants are able to absorb and store more water in their roots and therefore need less frequent watering.

2.4. Plant parts: Root, Leaf, Flower, and Fruit

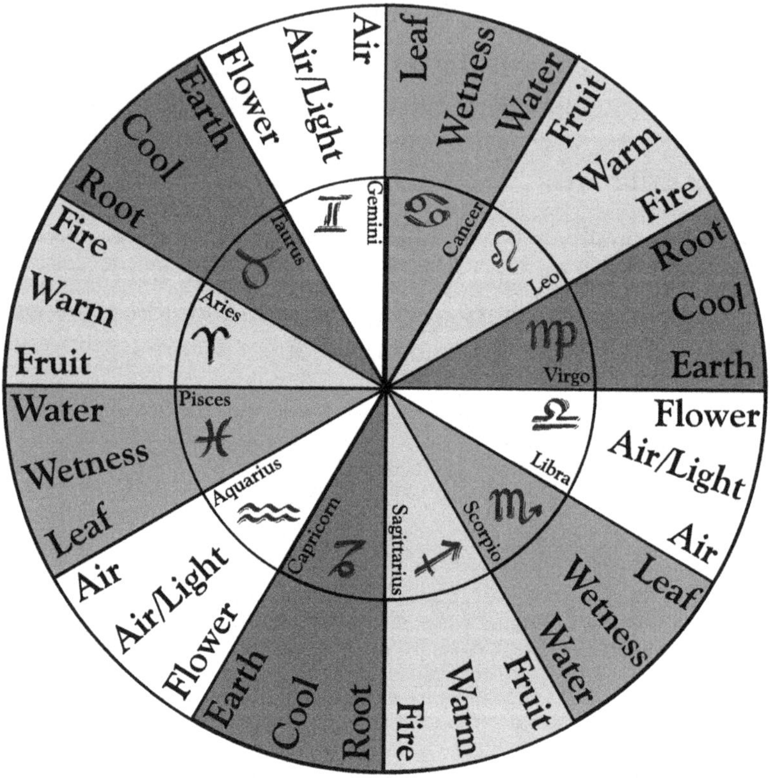

Fig. 2.c
The plant parts root, leaf, flower, and fruit are allocated to each zodiac sign according to the associated element.

According to each element, all parts of a plant are allocated to zodiac signs:

Aries, Leo, Sagittarius – Fire – WARM – Fruit

Taurus, Virgo, Capricorn – Earth – COOL – Root

Gemini, Libra, Aquarius – Air – AIR/LIGHT – Flower

Cancer, Scorpio, Pisces – Water – WETNESS – Leaf

The application can be summarized as follows. All measures for the growth and care of a certain plant part should be done on a day allocated to that plant part. Since tomatoes are fruit, to sow or plant tomatoes it is best to choose a fruit day such as when the moon travels in Aries, Leo, or Sagittarius. Leafy greens are best planted when the moon travels in Cancer, Scorpio, and Pisces, highlighting the leafy parts of plants. Root vegetables are best planted on a root day such as Taurus, Virgo, and Capricorn. When the moon concentrates its powers on the flower parts of a plant while traveling in Gemini, Libra, or Aquarius, planting flowers is most favorable.

Additions to this simple rule will be featured in chapter 3 respectively to the zodiac sign and the phase the moon is transiting.

2.5. Planting Time, Harvest Time, and Turning Points.

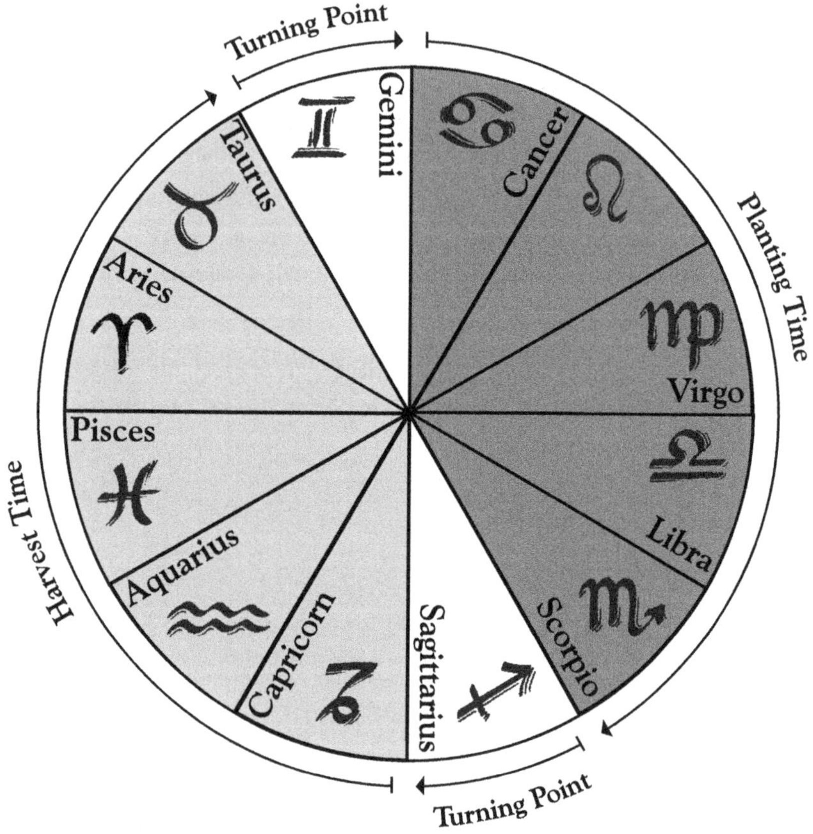

Fig. 2.d
Planting Time, Harvest Time, and Turning Points.

The classification of planting time, harvest time and turning points is linked with the ascending and descending forces of the moon during its travel through the zodiac signs.

Planting time. While the moon travels through the signs of Cancer, Leo, Virgo, Libra, and Scorpio, it displays descending forces which draw the sap downward in all plants, enhancing root formation. Hence these days are best for any sowing, planting, and transplanting of all plants as well harvesting of root plants.

Harvest time. During the time the moon travels in Capricorn, Aquarius, Pisces, Aries, and Taurus, the ascending forces are raising the sap in all plants upward, enhancing plant growth above ground and resulting in the most juicy fruits and vegetables. This is a good time for harvesting any plant that grows above ground and for harvesting fruit and vegetables for storage.

Turning points. Transitioning from ascending to descending forces and vice versa, both forces are at work, resulting in neutralizing effects on each other and preventing both harvesting and planting from yielding the best results.

Simultaneous with the ascending and descending forces, those of the waxing and waning moon are at work as well. During the waxing moon, sowing and planting plants that grow and flourish mostly above ground is best, while the forces of the waning moon support growth of plants below ground. Respective to the zodiac sign the moon is traveling through, the growth of roots, leaves, flowers, or fruits is benefited.

Due to the interplay of the above-mentioned forces, some days are best suited for certain gardening tasks. However, alternative days are also suitable. If you miss planting plants that grow mostly above ground during the waxing moon, you can do it during the planting time of the ascending forces.

2.6. Food Components (Protein, Salt, Fat, Carbohydrate)

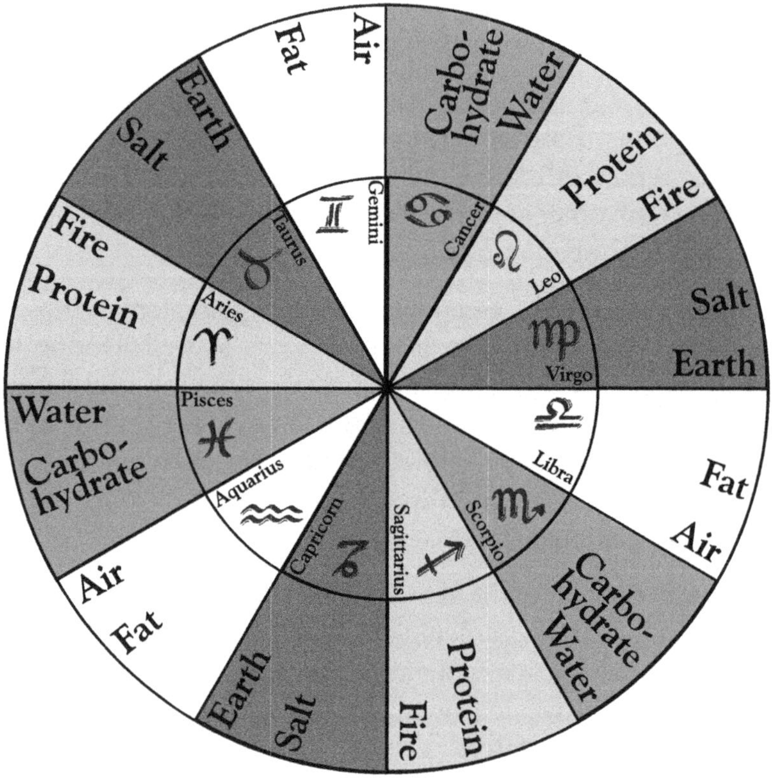

Fig 2.e
Food components (protein, salt, fat, and carbohydrate) correspond to the elements of the zodiac signs.

The food components of protein, salt, fat, and carbohydrate are linked to the elements of the zodiac signs on any given day. Healthy bodies absorb and digest the assigned food component the best, while sensitive or sick bodies may not fare well with the same food component. Observe how your body digests the assigned food components on any given day and factor this in for your choice of foods.

On a day when the element of air is prevalent, you might feel drawn to fatty meals and digest them very well. Fats support the glandular systems. If your glandular system is out of balance or malfunctioning, you may not digest fats well enough during these days even though you might feel drawn towards them. Consider that the less tired you feel after a meal, the better the choice and the quality of food was for your body.

On a day when carbohydrates are highlighted, some digest bread very well while others don't. On a day featuring the element of fire, WARM quality, and protein, some may digest protein extremely well and others may not. When salt is highlighted on a day linked to the element of earth, you might feel drawn to salty foods because the body will absorb salt better. Beware on these days if for health reasons you need to avoid salty foods.

If according to the lunar cycle you record your food intake, how you digest the food, your overall well-being, as well as which foods you feel drawn to, you will recognize your individual rhythm. This will make it easier and more efficient to plan your meals in support of your health while considering the lunar cycle and its effects.

2.7. Colors

When the sunlight shines through rain drops, the light rays can get separated into eight distinct light rays, which we see as a rainbow. All of the rainbow's colors are important for us. Just like sound, all colors have an effect on us. Colors can have healing effects, they can energize, harmonize, irritate, agitate, or have a depressing effect on us. Colors affect the psyche as well as the body. We choose or reject certain foods because of their color. We choose consciously or unconsciously colors that either strengthen or weaken us.

Colors apply to the lunar cycle and the position of the moon in each zodiac sign. They invite you to experience their influence on you on any given day of the lunar cycle. Do you feel comfortable wearing the color red while the moon is traveling in Scorpio? Or do you feel drawn to the contrasting color? Record your experiences with colors and their links to the zodiac signs, and you will develop a better intuition and feeling for which colors support you best.

Zodiac Sign	Color
Aries	Indigo Blue
Taurus	Bright Blue
Gemini	Light Blue
Cancer	Green
Leo	Green
Virgo	Yellow
Libra	Orange
Scorpio	Red
Sagittarius	Orange/Yellow
Capricorn	Yellow
Aquarius	Bright/Dark Blue
Pisces	Blueish White

2.8. Aromas and Scents

Each zodiac sign correlates to certain herbs and their aromas and scents. Whether you like to use them as aromatherapy oils, essences, or herbal teas, they can enhance your well being and support your health. It is interesting to observe their effect on you maybe you feel more drawn to scents of the earth element rather the than those of any other element? Or maybe you reject the scents of a certain element?

You can follow the list of aromas through the lunar cycle and drink some herbal teas accordingly. This way you treat your body to a wide variety of different herbs and their healing properties. Your body will use them depending on the waxing or waning moon to gather strength or to detoxify.

Zodiac Sign	Aromas and Scents
Aries	Cloves, Peppermint, Thyme
Taurus	Geranium, Jasmine, Rose
Gemini	Lavender, Lemon Balm, Magnolia, Verbena
Cancer	Lilac, Lilies of the Valley, Lilies, Violets
Leo	Hibiscus, Oleander, Rose
Virgo	Lavender, Fir, Sage, Meadow flowers
Libra	Roses, Violets, Daffodils
Scorpio	Anemone, Cornflower, Oregano, Thuja
Sagittarius	Marigold, Geranium, Rosemary
Capricorn	Cedar, Juniper
Aquarius	Cyclamen, Peach, Wild Roses
Pisces	Magnolia, Amaryllis, Clary Sage

2.9. Sensitive Body Parts

Each zodiac sign is the "ruler" of certain body parts, starting with the zodiac sign Aries' link to the head and ending with Pisces' link to the feet and toes. Therefore each lunar cycle while the moon is traveling through all the zodiac signs, every body part gets affected for 2-3 days. For the duration of these days the following **3 rules** apply:

1.

Every treatment and measure you undertake for the care and well-being of the body parts that are affected by the moon are more effective and beneficial. A foot massage during the days when the moon travels in Pisces is more beneficial than on the days when the moon travels in Aries. But there is one exception to this rule – if possible, avoid any surgery on the respective body parts that are affected by the moon, as well as on the respective body parts of the zodiac sign the sun is in.

2.

Beware that everything that puts a special burden or strain on the body parts affected by the lunar cycle is more harmful. If, for example, the moon is traveling through the zodiac sign of Scorpio, a slight hypothermia of the lower body can more quickly result in a bladder infection than on days the lunar cycle does not affect the urinary tract.

3.

During the waxing moon all measures taken to supply nutrient materials and strengthen the sensitive body parts are more effective. When the moon is on the wane, all measures taken to flush out and detoxify are more beneficial.

Every part of the body receives support from the forces of the lunar cycle. During half of the cycle these forces support any measures to detoxify the body parts; during the other half they support any measures to strengthen the body parts.

Zodiac Sign	Sensitive Body Parts
Aries	Head, Brain, Eyes
Taurus	Head and Neck
Gemini	Shoulders, Arms, Hands, and Lungs
Cancer	Chest, Lungs, Liver, Stomach, Gall Bladder
Leo	Heart, Back, Diaphragm, Circulation, Arteries
Virgo	Digestive Organs, Nerves, Spleen, Pancreas
Libra	Hips, Kidneys, and Bladder
Scorpio	Sex Organs, Ureter
Sagittarius	Thighs and Veins
Capricorn	Knees, Bones, Joints, Skin
Aquarius	Lower Legs and Veins
Pisces	Feet and Toes

Fig. 2.e
Each zodiac sign is linked to certain body parts.

3. The Effects of the Lunar Cycle on Daily Activities in Multiple Areas of Life

"There are journeys we need to make on our own,
with only the stars and moon to guide us,
maybe only after then
would we really discover our true potential."
Kelly Iyogun

The first chapter in this book illustrates the effects of the phases of the moon, New Moon, waxing moon, Full Moon, and waning moon. The second chapter explains the influence of the zodiac signs on the lunar cycle. Divided according to the zodiac and the waxing and waning moon, in this chapter all impacts mentioned previously are explained in detail as they affect the areas of **success, leisure, health, body care, garden/nature, housework,** and **nutrition.**

The various areas of life at a glance:

Success

Considering the effect of the lunar cycle enables you to plan ahead to best utilize all opportunities, possibilities, and activities. You may have experienced a great many times that on some days work goes easier and more efficiently than on other days.

Any financial matters are best dealt with on days when the moon travels in Taurus. Our perception is heightened and realistic, and financial security is of importance. Conservative tendencies make people want to stay away from risks.

Meetings that require negotiating, networking, and brainstorming are best scheduled on days when the influence of the moon traveling in Gemini supports communication, rather than on days when the Pisces influence makes retreat and fantasy more desirable than anything else.

Knowing the subtle influence of the lunar cycle, any goal-oriented activity can be scheduled optimally to avoid any negative influences and achieve the most successful results while saving time, effort, and money.

Leisure

What is the best day for a successful party event? During the days moon travels in Leo, people are most outgoing, favoring parties and other social events. It is advisable to avoid planning any activities outside the home when moon transits through Pisces, because at this time retreat and relaxation at home feels best.

Have more fun! Plan parties and activities when you and others enjoy them the most. Know in advance what will work best for family and social time, hobbies, exercises, and other leisure activities in life.

Health

The influence of the lunar cycle on each body part is explained in great detail in the second chapter. Support the sensitive body parts on the respective days, avoid any strain on them, and if possible avoid any surgery.

As the closing point of the preceding waning moon phase, New Moon is the culmination of the body's detoxification abilities and self-healing powers. Although healing powers are at their peak, any surgery should still be avoided if possible.

During the waxing moon everything that is supplied to the body to strengthen and build it up is more effective. Stimulants and vitamins are more potent. The closer it is to Full Moon, the stronger the impact of the forces will be. Counteract mineral and/or vitamin deficiencies in the body during the waxing moon. Supply your diet with supplements and herbs. Focus on foods that contain plenty of the minerals and vitamins your body needs.

Drugs also have a much stronger effect during the waxing moon. All measures taken to supply nutrient materials and strengthen the sensitive body parts are very effective. Healing ointments are absorbed well. Pay attention since the body also absorbs poisonous substances more easily. The body tends to retain water during this time, and diuretic measures don't work as well.

The closer it is to Full Moon, the more important it is to stay away from surgery if possible. Healing and recovery will take longer, and scarring will be more severe.

A day of fasting on a Full Moon day promotes health and can prevent illnesses. Be cautious and aware that since the body utilizes nutrition most effectively during this time, it acts the same on any artificial flavors, additives, stimulants, drugs as well as poisonous substances.

Wounds might bleed more profusely than at other times. Recovery after surgery is impeded. Vaccinations are unfavorable in the three days before and on Full Moon. Tissues are more likely to accumulate water.

When the moon is on the wane the body is ready to detoxify and cleanse. All measures taken to flush out and detoxify the sensitive body parts are very effective. The closer it is to New Moon, the stronger the waxing moon's impact will be. During the waning moon, any cleansing and detox diets will yield best results. Herbal teas, steam room, sauna... anything to detoxify and cleanse are best utilized between Full Moon and New Moon.

The body tends to heal faster during the waning moon and the success rates of surgeries are much higher. If you have the choice, schedule operations accordingly. Scarring is less severe, wounds are likely to bleed less during the waning moon, and surgical operations in general are less taxing on the body. To yield the best results, schedule dental treatments at this time, such as removal of tartar and amalgam as well as fillings, crowns, and dentures.

Body Care

You may have wondered why on some days your hair just doesn't retain its form, or why the same body treatments seem to yield different results on different days?

The lunar cycle has an effect on body, nail, and hair care. Massages are more effective during certain periods of the lunar cycle. Washing hair during the time the moon travels in Pisces may result in dandruff. Knowing all the details enables you to pick the best dates for your visit to the hair dresser. You will also save on hair restorers.

There is an old farmer's rule of cutting and filing fingernails and toenails any Friday after sunset. The result of that rule is healthy and strong nails.

Scents are assigned to each zodiac sign. Improve your well-being by surrounding yourself with these soothing scents.

Garden/Nature

The lunar cycle has an effect on each part of a plant: roots, leaves, fruits or blossoms. Pick the right timing for great results. For example, when planting leafy vegetables such as lettuce, spinach or cabbage, choose a leaf day for best results. For any root vegetables such as carrots, beets, radishes, choose a root day. You will find the categorization of the most common vegetables below in figure 3.a.

If you consider the lunar effect on plants, your plants will grow better, your harvest will be plentiful, and pests will be reduced or completely avoided. Weeding, fertilizing, and watering will be less frequent but more effective.

There are many opportunities to coordinate your agenda for the kind of work you want to do. Consider as well that on New Moon and Full Moon weather changes are more likely.

If you want to collect healing herbs when they have maximum healing power, pick the days of the full moon or the days on which the lunar cycle highlights the body parts that the healing herbs will benefit. For example, to pick herbs that help with bladder and kidney infections collect the herbs on a day when the moon travels in Libra and the bladder and kidneys are most sensitive.

Some days are the most unfavorable for any gardening activities. These days occur about twice a month, the day after the moon crosses the earth's equator.

Housework

Doing housework in tune with nature and the lunar cycle will get you the best results for your efforts. It's like magic!

Housework is dealt with much more successfully, efficiently, and effortlessly during the waning moon. For example, problem stains are removed readily. Reduce your use of cleaners and save money. You will also be supporting the environment, since waste water is broken down much better. Get the best results with baking, cooking, and preserving foods.

Improve and refine your methods. Use the most favorable time for your work and visible results will be proof of your success, saving you time for the things you enjoy most.

Nutrition

Discover simple ways to improve your diet. Know which fruits and vegetables benefit your body the most. Eat anything you like, but optimize the timing!

The food components of protein, salt, fat, and carbohydrate are linked to the elements of the zodiac signs on any given day. Healthy bodies absorb and digest the assigned food component the best, while sensitive or sick bodies may not fare well with the same food component. Observe how your body digests the assigned food components on any given day and factor this in for your choice of foods.

According to each element, all plant parts are linked to zodiac signs. When the moon travels in Aries, Leo, and Sagittarius, all plants that are fruits are highlighted, and correspondingly our bodies digest fruits the best. The same logic applies when the moon travels in Taurus, Virgo, and Capricorn and roots are highlighted – our bodies digest root vegetables the best. When the moon travels in Gemini, Libra, and Aquarius, we digest all plant that are flowers the best, like artichokes, cauliflower, and broccoli. On days the moon transits through Cancer, Scorpio, and Pisces we benefit from eating leafy vegetables.

Plant Parts	Zodiac Signs	Fruits and Vegetables
Fruit	Aries Leo Sagittarius	beans, peas, corn, tomatoes, pumpkin, lentils, soybeans, cucumber, eggplant, zucchini, berries, fruit, chili, bell pepper, figs, avocado, melon, olives
Root	Taurus Virgo Capricorn	garlic, carrots, red beets, radish, rutabaga, sugar beet, celery, potatoes, onions, kohlrabi
Flower	Gemini Libra Aquarius	cauliflower, artichoke, broccoli, sunflower seeds, flax seeds, nuts, rose hip, elder
Leaf	Cancer Scorpio Pisces	lettuce, spinach, lamb's lettuce, Endive, parsley, leek, cabbage (Brussels sprouts, kale, Chinese cabbage), all leafy herbs, asparagus, mushrooms, cress, Swiss chard, rhubarb

Fig. 3.a
Classification of vegetables linked to plant parts and zodiac signs.

The waning and waxing moon phases influence both weight gain and weight loss. During the waxing moon, the body readily absorbs and you are more likely to gain weight even with regular amounts of food intake. Therefore it is advisable to avoid indulging in rich foods. If you are overweight, eat smaller portions. During the waning moon, the body is ready to detoxify and cleanse, and weight gain associated with overeating is less likely. Anybody underweight should consider eating larger portions.

During the waxing moon, everything that is supplied to the body to build up and strengthen is much more effective. Stimulants and vitamins have a stronger effect. The closer it is to Full Moon, the stronger the waning moon phase's impact will be. In contrast, during waning moon all measures taken to flush out and detoxify the sensitive body parts are very effective. The closer to New Moon the stronger the impact of the forces. During waning moon any cleansing and detox diets will yield the best results. Herbal teas, steam room, sauna... anything to detoxify and cleanse are best utilized between Full Moon and New Moon.

Since the Internal Organ Clock pictured in the foreword of this reference book indicates that the kidneys are activated by the meridians between 5pm to 7pm daily, it's beneficial for your kidneys and overall health to drink a lot of water during this specific time.

3.1. Moon in Aries

Element	Plant Part	Gardening	Sensitive Body Parts	Food Component
Fire – Warm	**Fruit**	**Harvest Time**	**Head, Brain, and Eyes**	**Protein**

(Chapter 2.1. features the general description of each zodiac sign.)

Success

With Aries, determination, drive, and initiative, things get going and the way straight ahead seems the best.

People feel energetic, courageous, assertive, and at times anxious.

It's a good time for meetings and sales talks but keep in mind that impatience, single-mindedness and selfishness do not favor teamwork.

Leisure Time

An enterprising spirit and spontaneity move people to enjoy outings, sports, competitions, cultural events, and travels.

Romance can be very passionate, for Aries represents the element of fire.

These are in general good days for outings, and even with cloudy skies the air still feels somewhat warm. But a drying effect will make you more thirsty and dehydrated, so make sure you get plenty to drink.

☽ Waxing Moon in Aries

Now is the best time to start anything new or alter, reconfigure, and remodel in many areas such as on the job, at school, for leisure, and in the home. It is essential to focus and gather forces, getting plenty of time to rest, recover, regroup, and gain new

 ♈

strength. The closer it is to Full Moon, the stronger the impact of the forces will be.

Health During Waxing Moon in Aries ☽

Healing ointments are easily absorbed. All measures taken to supply nutrient materials and strengthen the sensitive body parts of the head, brain, and eyes are very effective.

Consider that the sense organs are more sensitive as well.

Since the head is more sensitive, if you suffer from migraines drink plenty of water, and avoid coffee, chocolate, and sugar during these days.

Close to Full Moon any surgery should be avoided if possible, since the healing process slows down and scarring can be more severe.

Body Care During Waxing Moon in Aries ☽

All measures taken to supply nutrient materials and strengthen the body are very effective. Treatments with firming and moisturizing creams are more effective as well as massages to regenerate and strengthen, perhaps added with beneficial massage oils. Since Aries affects the head and eyes, this is a good time for any facial treatments, massages, and eye compresses for strained eyes.

Correcting and cutting ingrown nails during these days promotes healthy growth.

Any kind of hair care works well and hair dyes will look more vibrant.

Enjoy the scents of cloves, peppermint, and thyme.

Garden/Nature During Waxing Moon in Aries ☽

When the moon travels in Aries, any garden work benefiting fruits is most effective. Sow plants and vegetables that grow and flourish above ground, especially fruit and tomatoes. In the appropriate season grafting onto fruit trees is more successful when moon travels in Aries.

Furthermore, it is recommended to sow and plant anything that is supposed to grow fast and for immediate use.

Cultivating grains is also favorable while the moon is in Aries.

Transplanting yields good results.

Harvest time is here with ascending forces! Sap is rising, enhancing plant growth above ground, and fruits and vegetables are at their most juicy. Harvesting and storing grains, vegetables, potatoes, fruit, and tomatoes is recommended.

Since Aries affects the head and eyes, gather herbs for eye complaints and headaches.

Housework During Waxing Moon in Aries ☽

If you intend to remodel or rearrange furniture, start during the waxing moon phase. However, only light housework is advisable, since the waxing moon still requires time to relax, recover, and gather strength.

Every time the moon travels through a star sign that represents the element of fire, it's best to ventilate rooms sufficiently since the air in general is not as humid.

The element of fire makes baking yield good results. Dough for breads, cakes, and cookies rises faster, except on the days close to New Moon. Making cheese is also suitable during these days.

When the moon travels in Aries, anything pertaining to fruits is favorable, such as preserving and freezing.

Nutrition During Waxing Moon in Aries ☽

Everything that is supplied to the body to build up and strengthen is most effective. Stimulants and vitamins have a stronger effect.

Any deficiencies of minerals and/or vitamins in the body are best taken care of during the waxing moon. Include all important supplements, tonics, and herbs in your diet. Focus on foods that contain essential minerals and vitamins your body is lacking.

Since the body readily absorbs at this time, you are more likely to gain weight even with a regular amount of food intake. Therefore avoid indulging in rich foods. If you are overweight, eat smaller portions.

Drugs have a much stronger effect. All measures taken to supply nutrient materials and strengthen the sensitive body parts are very effective. Be aware that the body also more readily absorbs poisonous substances. The body retains water more easily, and diuretic measures don't work as effectively.

While the moon travels in Aries, pay attention to proteins in your diet, especially if you don't digest them well during these days. Drink plenty of water, and keep your body well hydrated.

Include fruits in your meals. The fresh harvest on Aries days is very juicy, and the body digests fruits the best at this time.

☾ Waning Moon in Aries

Now it's time to be active, detoxify, and remove. If your schedule is flexible, plan your activities during the waning moon phase, because you will reach your goals sooner and more easily, yielding better results.

Health During Waning Moon in Aries ☾

All measures taken to flush out and detoxify the sensitive body parts are very effective. During the waning moon any cleansing and detox diets will yield the best results. Herbal teas, steam room, sauna... anything to detox and cleanse are best utilized between Full Moon and New Moon. The closer to New Moon the stronger the impact of the forces.

♈ 

The body tends to heal faster during the waning moon and the success rates for surgeries are higher. If you have the choice, schedule surgery, except on the sensitive body parts such as head, brain, and eyes, as well as on the respective body parts of the zodiac sign the sun is in. Scarring is less severe, wounds most likely bleed less than during waxing moon, and surgical operations in general are less strenuous on the body. To yield best results schedule dental treatments such as removal of tartar and amalgam as well as fillings, crowns, and dentures. Avoid treatment of periodontitis and gums.

In addition to the head region, the sense organs are more sensitive as well.

If you suffer from migraines or frequent headaches, drink lots of water, and avoid coffee, chocolate, and sugar during these days.

Body Care During Waning Moon in Aries ☾

All measures taken to flush out and detoxify are very effective. The closer to New Moon the stronger the impact of the forces.

Apply detoxing facial and body care, treatments of bumps and pimples on the skin, and exfoliating procedures.

Prepare homemade ointments and cosmetics.

Remove body hair; it won't grow back as quickly. Removal of callused skin works best now.

Correction of the nail bed is advisable. Treatment of obstinate athlete's foot, nail fungus, and warts yields good results.

Massages that serve to relax, ease tension, and detoxify are most effective, such as reflexology massage.

Since Aries affects the head and eyes, this is a good time for eye compresses to relieve strained eyes.

Any kind of hair care yields good results.

Enjoy the scents of cloves, peppermint, and thyme.

Garden/Nature During Waning Moon in Aries ☾

The waning moon favors sowing and planting of plants and vegetables that grow below ground as well as weeding, pest control, fertilizing, spreading manure, and pruning trees and bushes.

When the moon travels in Aries, any garden work benefiting fruits is most effective. Therefore sowing and planting fruit and tomatoes, fertilizing grains, vegetables, and fruit, and pruning of fruit trees yields good results.

It is favorable to sow and plant anything that is supposed to grow fast and to set up a compost heap.

Dig over/plow the soil to prepare for planting.

Transplanting yields good results.

Harvest time is here with ascending forces! Sap is rising, enhancing plant growth above ground, and fruits and vegetables are at their most juicy. Harvesting and storing grains, vegetables, potatoes, fruit, and tomatoes is recommended.

Since Aries affects the head and eyes, gather herbs for eye complaints and headaches.

Housework During Waning Moon in Aries ☾

Housework is dealt with much more successfully, efficiently, and effortlessly during the waning moon. The cleansing effect on nature extends beyond our bodies into the environment. Problem stains are removed readily. Dirt and pollution are best dealt with during waning moon. Any dirt and spots are removed easily in the laundry, in all areas of house cleaning, at the car wash and in dry cleaning. Reduce on cleaners and save money. Support the environment since waste water is broken down much better.

Clean and store seasonal clothing now.

Thoroughly clean wooden and parquet floors, metals, china, etc.

Cleaning windows and glass is less likely to produce annoying streaks.

Cleaning, polishing, and waterproofing shoes works best.

Combating mold is more effective.

Every time the moon travels through a star sign that represents the element of fire, it's best to ventilate rooms sufficiently since the air in general is not as humid. Air bedding and mattresses also.

When moon travels in Aries anything pertaining to fruits is favorable, such as preserving and freezing. These days are suitable for making cheese.

Use of more leavening agent is advisable for baking bread, cakes, and cookies.

Good days for painting because the paint dries more quickly and bonds better.

Nutrition During Waning Moon in Aries ☾

The body is ready to detoxify and cleanse, and weight gain associated with overeating is less likely. Anybody underweight should consider eating larger portions.

All measures taken to flush out and detoxify the sensitive body parts are very effective. The closer to New Moon the stronger the impact of the forces. During the waning moon any cleansing and detox diets will yield the best results. Flush out poisonous substances. Treatment for drug abuse is most effective.

While the moon travels in Aries, pay attention to proteins in your diet, especially if you don't digest them well during these days. Drink plenty of water, and keep your body well hydrated.

Include fruits in your meals. The fresh harvest on Aries days is very juicy, and the body digests fruits the best at this time.

3.2. Moon in Taurus

Element	Plant Part	Gardening	Sensitive Body Parts	Food Component
Earth – Cool	**Root**	**Harvest Time**	**Head and Neck**	**Salt**

(Chapter 2.1. features the general description of each zodiac sign.)

Success

After the heady impatience of Aries, persistence comes easy, and thoughts and reactions are slower. Realism and material security are important. Conservative tendencies may make people want to stay away from risk taking. Assess financial areas now.

Leisure Time

Relax at a picnic/feast. Enjoy culinary pleasures and hobbies.

The earth feels cold to the touch, so take slightly warmer clothes.

☽ Waxing Moon in Taurus

Now is the best time to start anything new or alter, reconfigure, and remodel in many areas such as on the job, at school, for leisure, and in the home. It is essential to focus and gather forces, getting plenty of time to rest, recover, regroup, and gain new strength. The closer it is to Full Moon, the stronger the impact of the forces will be.

Health During Waxing Moon in Taurus ☽

Healing ointments are easily absorbed. All measures taken to supply nutrient materials and strengthen the sensitive body parts of the head and neck are very effective.

Consider that the blood circulation is more sensitive.

Organs of speech, jaws, teeth, tonsils, thyroid gland, neck, and vocal chords get easily affected. Keep the neck warm. On cold days

the ears should be protected. Some people experience more sensitivity to noise.

If you have high blood pressure, avoid salty foods.

Massages, lymphatic therapy, and chiropractic treatment to release blockages are beneficial.

Close to Full Moon any surgery should be avoided if possible, since the healing process slows down and scarring can be more severe.

Body Care During Waxing Moon in Taurus ☽

All measures taken to supply nutrient materials and strengthen the body are very effective. Treatments with firming and moisturizing creams are more effective as well as massages to regenerate and strengthen, perhaps added with beneficial massage oils.

Correcting and cutting ingrown nails during these days promotes healthy growth.

Hair dyes will look more vibrant.

Enjoy the scents of geranium, jasmine, and rose.

Garden/Nature During Waxing Moon in Taurus ☽

When the moon travels in Taurus, any garden work benefiting roots is most effective. Sow plants and vegetables that grow and flourish above ground, trees, bushes, hedges, and root vegetables. Everything grows slowly and lasts well.

Transplanting yields good results.

This is harvest time with ascending forces! Sap is rising, enhancing plant growth above ground, and fruits and vegetables are at their most juicy. Harvesting and storing root vegetables is recommended, because the harvested produce is especially suitable for storage.

Gather herbs for sinus issues, sore throat, and ear complaints.

Housework During Waxing Moon in Taurus ☽

If you intend to remodel or rearrange furniture, start during the waxing moon phase. However, only light housework is advisable, since the waxing moon still requires time to relax, recover, and gather strength.

Since Taurus is linked with the element of earth, we easily feel chilly. Therefore air rooms only briefly.

Preserving root vegetables yields good results.

Nutrition During Waxing Moon in Taurus ☽

Everything that is supplied to the body to build up and strengthen is most effective. Stimulants and vitamins have a stronger effect. Any deficiencies of minerals and/or vitamins in the body are best taken care of during the waxing moon. Include all important supplements, tonics, and herbs in your diet. Focus on foods that contain essential minerals and vitamins your body is lacking.

Since the body readily absorbs at this time, you are more likely to gain weight even with a regular amount of food intake. Therefore avoid indulging in rich foods. If you are overweight, eat smaller portions.

Drugs have a much stronger effect. All measures taken to supply nutrient materials and strengthen the sensitive body parts are very effective. Be aware that the body also more readily absorbs poisonous substances. The body retains water more easily, and diuretic measures don't work as effectively.

While the moon travels in Taurus, pay attention to the amount of salt in your diet. Avoid large quantities of salty foods like bacon, ham, salted herring, fatty cheese, and the like.

Include root vegetables in your meals, as the body digests them very well now.

☾ Waning Moon in Taurus

Now it's time to be active, detoxify, and remove. If your schedule is flexible, plan your activities during the waning moon phase, because you will reach your goals sooner and more easily, yielding better results.

Health During Waning Moon in Taurus ☾

All measures taken to flush out and detoxify the sensitive body parts are very effective. During the waning moon any cleansing and detox diets will yield the best results. Herbal teas, steam room, sauna... anything to detox and cleanse are best utilized between Full Moon and New Moon. The closer to New Moon the stronger the impact of the forces.

The body tends to heal faster during the waning moon and the success rates for surgeries are higher. If you have the choice, schedule surgery, except on the sensitive body parts such as head, and neck, as well as on the respective body parts of the zodiac sign the sun is in. Scarring is less severe, wounds most likely bleed less than during waxing moon, and surgical operations in general are less strenuous on the body. To yield best results schedule dental treatments such as removal of tartar and amalgam as well as fillings, crowns, and dentures. Avoid treatment of periodontitis and gums.

Blood-purifying and detoxifying herbal infusions and teas are most beneficial.

Consider that the blood circulation is more sensitive.

Organs of speech, jaws, teeth, tonsils, thyroid gland, neck, and vocal chords get easily affected. Keep the neck warm. On cold days the ears should be protected. Some people experience more sensitivity to noise.

If you have high blood pressure, avoid salty foods.

Massages, lymphatic therapy, and chiropractic treatment to release blockages are beneficial.

 ♉

Body Care During Waning Moon in Taurus ☾

All measures taken to flush out and detoxify are very effective. The closer to New Moon the stronger the impact of the forces.

Apply detoxing facial and body care, treatments of bumps and pimples on the skin, and exfoliating procedures.

Prepare homemade ointments and cosmetics.

Remove body hair; it won't grow back as quickly. Removal of callused skin works best now.

Correction of the nail bed is advisable. Treatment of obstinate athlete's foot, nail fungus, and warts yields good results.

Massages that serve to relax, ease tension, and detoxify are most effective, such as reflexology massage.

Enjoy the scents of geranium, jasmine and rose.

Garden/Nature During Waning Moon in Taurus ☾

The waning moon in Taurus favors sowing and planting of plants and vegetables that grow below ground as well as weeding and mulching. Everything grows slowly and lasts well.

Dig over the soil to prepare for planting. Trimming and cutting back plants will favor healthy growth.

Combat vermin found in the soil. Spread fertilizer and liquid manure. Fertilize flowers with poorly formed roots. Start a compost heap if needed.

This is harvest time with ascending forces! Sap is rising, enhancing plant growth above ground, fruits and vegetables are at their most juicy. Harvested produce is well suited for storage. Harvesting root vegetables is recommended.

Gather herbs (roots) for sinus issues, sore throat, and ear complaints.

♉ 

Housework During Waning Moon in Taurus ☾

Housework is dealt with much more successfully, efficiently, and effortlessly during the waning moon. The cleansing effect on nature extends beyond our bodies into the environment. Problem stains are removed readily. Dirt and pollution are best dealt with during waning moon. Any dirt and spots are removed easily in the laundry, in all areas of house cleaning, at the car wash and in dry cleaning. Reduce on cleaners and save money. Support the environment since waste water is broken down much better.

Clean and store seasonal clothing now.

Thoroughly clean wooden and parquet floors, metals, china, etc.

Cleaning, polishing, and waterproofing shoes works best.

Combating mold is more effective.

Since Taurus is linked with the element of earth, we easily feel chilly. Therefore air rooms only briefly.

Preserving root vegetables yields good results.

Good days for painting because the paint dries more quickly and bonds better.

Nutrition During Waning Moon in Taurus ☾

During waning moon the body is ready to detoxify and cleanse, and weight gain associated with overeating is less likely. Anybody underweight should consider eating larger portions.

All measures taken to flush out and detoxify the sensitive body parts are very effective. The closer to New Moon the stronger the impact of the forces. During the waning moon any cleansing and detox diets will yield the best results. Flush out poisonous substances. Treatment for drug abuse is most effective.

While the moon travels in Taurus, pay attention to the amount of salt in your diet. Avoid large quantities of salty foods like bacon, ham, salted herring, fatty cheese, and the like.

Include root vegetables in your meals, as the body digests them very well now.

3.3. Moon in Gemini

Element	Plant Part	Gardening	Sensitive Body Parts	Food Component
Air – Light	**Flower**	**Turning Point**	**Shoulders, Arms, Hands, and Lungs**	**Fat**

(Chapter 2.1. features the general description of each zodiac sign.)

Success

The stability of Taurus will turn into a changeable and hectic time while the moon is in Gemini. Open-mindedness and curiosity reign. This is a good time for talking, negotiating, networking, and exchanging ideas as well as for meetings of a nonbinding nature, conferences, and studies.

Leisure Time

People enjoy stimulating their minds with reading and studying. Attending theater performances is a preferred enjoyment now.

Enhance your friendships. This is a good time for family gatherings, parties, and short trips. Plan for some stretching exercises also.

Be prepared for sudden changes in weather or climate.

☽ Waxing Moon in Gemini

Now is the best time to start anything new or alter, reconfigure, and remodel in many areas such as on the job, at school, for leisure, and in the home. It is essential to focus and gather forces, getting plenty of time to rest, recover, regroup, and gain new strength. The closer it is to Full Moon, the stronger the impact of the forces will be.

Health During Waxing Moon in Gemini ☽

Healing ointments are easily absorbed. All measures taken to supply nutrient materials and strengthen the sensitive body parts of the shoulders, arms, hands, and lungs are very effective.

Consider that the glandular system is more sensitive.

If possible avoid having any teeth pulled.

Exercises for shoulders and breathing exercises are most beneficial.

Make sure you are dressed warm enough in cool weather. People are more sensitive to light, so bring your sunglasses along when staying outside.

Massages, lymphatic therapy, and chiropractic treatment to release blockages are beneficial.

Close to Full Moon any surgery should be avoided if possible, since the healing process slows down and scarring can be more severe.

Body Care During Waxing Moon in Gemini ☽

All measures taken to supply nutrient materials and strengthen the body are very effective. Treatments with firming and moisturizing creams are more effective as well as massages to regenerate and strengthen, perhaps added with beneficial massage oils.

Correcting and cutting ingrown nails during these days promotes healthy growth.

Hair dyes will look more vibrant.

Enjoy the scents of lavender, lemon balm, magnolia, and verbena.

Garden/Nature During Waxing Moon in Gemini ☽

When the moon travels in Gemini, any garden work benefiting the flower part of a plant is most effective. Sow plants and vegetables that grow and flourish above ground, creeping or climbing plants, flowers, and medicinal herbs.

Transplanting yields good results.

Avoid watering plants, as it attracts pests.

This is a turning point. Whether transitioning from ascending to descending forces or vice versa, both forces are at work and neutralize each other. As a result, neither harvesting nor planting yields best results.

Gather herbs for tensions in the shoulder and lung complaints.

Changes in weather are more likely.

Housework During Waxing Moon in Gemini

If you intend to remodel or rearrange furniture, start during the waxing moon phase. However, only light housework is advisable, since the waxing moon still requires time to relax, recover, and gather strength.

Because Gemini is linked to the element of air, ventilate rooms thoroughly.

Making preserves yields good results.

It is a good time for baking cakes and cookies, because the dough rises faster, except on New Moon.

Nutrition During Waxing Moon in Gemini

Everything that is supplied to the body to build up and strengthen is most effective. Stimulants and vitamins have a stronger effect. Any deficiencies of minerals and/or vitamins in the body are best taken care of during the waxing moon. Include all important supplements, tonics, and herbs in your diet. Focus on foods that contain essential minerals and vitamins your body is lacking.

Since the body readily absorbs at this time, you are more likely to gain weight even with a regular amount of food intake. Therefore avoid indulging in rich foods. If you are overweight, eat smaller portions.

Drugs have a much stronger effect. All measures taken to supply nutrient materials and strengthen the sensitive body parts are very effective. Be aware that the body also more readily absorbs poisonous substances. The body retains water more easily, and diuretic measures don't work as effectively.

While the moon travels in Gemini, pay attention to the fats in your diet and to any particularly tempting foods today. Most likely the "wrong" things taste best.

If you have high cholesterol eat a low fat diet.

Include flower vegetables in your meals, as the body digests them very well now.

☾ Waning Moon in Gemini

Now it's time to be active, detoxify, and remove. If your schedule is flexible, plan your activities during the waning moon phase, because you will reach your goals sooner and more easily, yielding better results.

Health During Waning Moon in Gemini ☾

All measures taken to flush out and detoxify the sensitive body parts are very effective. During the waning moon any cleansing and detox diets will yield the best results. Herbal teas, steam room, sauna... anything to detox and cleanse are best utilized between Full Moon and New Moon. The closer to New Moon the stronger the impact of the forces.

The body tends to heal faster during the waning moon and the success rates for surgeries are higher. If you have the choice, schedule surgery, except on the sensitive body parts such as shoulders, arms, hands, and lungs, as well as on the respective body parts of the zodiac sign the sun is in. Scarring is less severe, wounds most likely bleed less than during waxing moon, and surgical operations in general are less strenuous on the body. To yield best results schedule dental treatments such as removal of tartar and amalgam as well as fillings, crowns, and dentures. If possible avoid having any teeth pulled.

Blood-purifying and detoxifying herbal infusions and teas are most beneficial.

 ♊

Consider that the glandular system is more sensitive.

If possible avoid having any teeth pulled.

Exercises for shoulders and breathing exercises are most beneficial.

Make sure you are dressed warm enough in cool weather. People are more sensitive to light, so bring your sunglasses along when staying outside.

Massages, lymphatic therapy, and chiropractic treatment to release blockages are beneficial.

Close to Full Moon any surgery should be avoided if possible, since the healing process slows down and scarring can be more severe.

Body Care During Waning Moon in Gemini ☾

All measures taken to flush out and detoxify are very effective. The closer to New Moon the stronger the impact of the forces.

Apply detoxing facial and body care, treatments of bumps and pimples on the skin, and exfoliating procedures.

Prepare homemade ointments and cosmetics.

Remove body hair; it won't grow back as quickly. Removal of callused skin works best now.

Correction of the nail bed is advisable. Treatment of obstinate athlete's foot, nail fungus, and warts yields good results.

Massages that serve to relax, ease tension, and detoxify are most effective, such as reflexology massage.

Enjoy the scents of lavender, lemon balm, magnolia, and verbena.

Garden/Nature During Waning Moon in Gemini ☾

The waning moon in Gemini favors sowing and planting of plants and vegetables that grow below ground as well as weeding and pest control.

Trimming and cutting back plants will favor healthy growth.

Avoid watering plants, as it attracts pests.

This is a turning point. Whether transitioning from ascending to descending forces or vice versa, both forces are at work and neutralize each other. As a result, neither harvesting nor planting yields best results.

Gather herbs for tensions in the shoulder and lung complaints.

Changes in weather are more likely.

Housework During Waning Moon in Gemini ☾

Housework is dealt with much more successfully, efficiently, and effortlessly during the waning moon. The cleansing effect on nature extends beyond our bodies into the environment. Problem stains are removed readily. Dirt and pollution are best dealt with during waning moon. Any dirt and spots are removed easily in the laundry, in all areas of house cleaning, at the car wash and in dry cleaning. Reduce on cleaners and save money. Support the environment since waste water is broken down much better.

Clean and store seasonal clothing now.

Thoroughly clean wooden and parquet floors, metals, china, etc.

Cleaning windows and glass is less likely to produce annoying streaks.

Cleaning, polishing, and waterproofing shoes works best.

Combating mold is more effective.

Because Gemini is linked to the element of air, ventilate rooms thoroughly.

Making preserves yields good results.

It is a good time for baking bread, cakes, and cookies if more leavening agent is added to the dough.

Nutrition During Waning Moon in Gemini ☾

During waning moon the body is ready to detoxify and cleanse, and weight gain associated with overeating is less likely. Anybody underweight should consider eating larger portions.

All measures taken to flush out and detoxify the sensitive body parts are very effective. The closer to New Moon the stronger the impact of the forces. During the waning moon any cleansing and detox diets will yield the best results. Flush out poisonous substances. Treatment for drug abuse is most effective.

While the moon travels in Gemini, pay attention to the fats in your diet and to any particularly tempting foods today. Most likely the "wrong" things taste best.

If you have high cholesterol eat a low fat diet.

Include flower vegetables in your meals, as the body digests them very well now.

3.4. Moon in Cancer

Element	Plant Part	Gardening	Sensitive Body Parts	Food Component
Water – Wetness	**Leaf**	**Planting Time**	**Chest, Lungs, Liver, Stomach, and Gall Bladder**	**Carbohydrate**

(Chapter 2.1. features the general description of each zodiac sign.)

Success

Feelings, sensitivity, and cooperativeness are in the foreground. Many are overly sensitive, so beware of treading on someone's toes. Be cautious if you are easily influenced; remember to consider your own goals.

During negotiations make use of the cognitive ability of your senses.

Leisure Time

The inner world becomes more colorful than the outer. Relax within your close family. Retreat to your safe haven and enjoy your fantasy while reading or listening to music.

Romance can be gentle. Deep feelings will prevail.

If you plan outdoor excursions, be prepared for a shower here and there.

☽ Waxing Moon in Cancer

Now is the best time to start anything new or alter, reconfigure, and remodel in many areas such as on the job, at school, for leisure, and in the home. It is essential to focus and gather forces, getting plenty of time to rest, recover, regroup, and gain new strength. The closer it is to Full Moon, the stronger the impact of the forces will be.

Health During Waxing Moon in Cancer ☽

Healing ointments are easily absorbed. All measures taken to supply nutrient materials and strengthen the sensitive body parts of the chest, lungs, liver, stomach, and gall bladder are very effective.

Consider that the nervous system is more sensitive.

Be cautious with alcohol since the liver is very sensitive.

The stomach could play up and cause gas and heartburn.

If you suffer from rheumatism, don't air bedding outside, because the damp will remain in the bedding.

Lymphatic therapy is most beneficial.

Close to Full Moon any surgery should be avoided if possible, since the healing process slows down and scarring can be more severe.

Body Care During Waxing Moon in Cancer ☽

All measures taken to supply nutrient materials and strengthen the body are very effective. Treatments with firming and moisturizing creams are more effective as well as massages that serve to regenerate, and strengthen, perhaps with the aid of appropriate oils.

Correcting and cutting ingrown nails during these days promotes healthy growth.

Avoid washing your hair and avoid any haircuts during Cancer days, because hair becomes shaggy and unmanageable.

Enjoy the scents of lilac, lilies of the valley, lilies, and violets.

Garden/Nature During Waxing Moon in Cancer ☽

When the moon travels in Cancer, any garden work benefiting the leaves of a plant is most effective. Sow plants and vegetables that grow and flourish above ground, any leaf vegetables, but no lettuce.

Transplanting yields good results.

Water all indoor and outdoor plants. The roots absorb and store more water and as a result will need less frequent watering.

Trimming and cutting back plants will result in healthy growth. But avoid pruning fruit trees and bushes.

Cut trees, garlands, and pick flowers to dry; they will last longer.

Sowing and mowing lawns is favorable during these days.

Start a compost heap if needed.

This is a planting time with descending forces. Sap is drawn downward, enhancing root formation. Avoid any harvesting, storing and preserving.

Gather herbs for bronchitis, stomach, liver, and gall bladder complaints.

Housework During Waxing Moon in Cancer ☽

If you intend to remodel or rearrange furniture, start during the waxing moon phase. However, only light housework is advisable, since the waxing moon still requires time to relax, recover, and gather strength.

Because Cancer is linked to the element of water, ventilate rooms briefly and rapidly. Don't air any mattresses.

Any dirt and spots are easily removed in the laundry.

Avoid painting, as paint will take very long to dry.

Nutrition During Waxing Moon in Cancer ☽

Everything that is supplied to the body to build up and strengthen is most effective. Stimulants and vitamins have a stronger effect. Any deficiencies of minerals and/or vitamins in the body are best taken care of during the waxing moon. Include all important supplements, tonics, and herbs in your diet. Focus on foods that contain essential minerals and vitamins your body is lacking.

 ♋

Since the body readily absorbs at this time, you are more likely to gain weight even with a regular amount of food intake. Therefore avoid indulging in rich foods. If you are overweight, eat smaller portions.

Drugs have a much stronger effect. All measures taken to supply nutrient materials and strengthen the sensitive body parts are very effective. Be aware that the body also more readily absorbs poisonous substances. The body retains water more easily, and diuretic measures don't work as effectively.

While the moon travels in Cancer, pay attention to the carbohydrates in your diet.

Moodiness may make you want to eat more than is healthy. If you get stomach troubles easily, avoid heavy meals.

Include leafy vegetables in your meals, as the body digests them very well now.

☾ Waning Moon in Cancer

Now it's time to be active, detoxify, and remove. If your schedule is flexible, plan your activities during the waning moon phase, because you will reach your goals sooner and more easily, yielding better results.

Health During Waning Moon in Cancer ☾

All measures taken to flush out and detoxify the sensitive body parts are very effective. During the waning moon any cleansing and detox diets will yield the best results. Herbal teas, steam room, sauna... anything to detox and cleanse are best utilized between Full Moon and New Moon. The closer to New Moon the stronger the impact of the forces.

The body tends to heal faster during the waning moon and the success rates for surgeries are higher. If you have the choice, schedule surgery, except on the sensitive body parts such as chest, lungs, liver, stomach, and gall bladder, as well as on the respective body parts of the zodiac sign the sun is in. Scarring is less severe, wounds most likely bleed less than during waxing moon, and surgical operations in general are less strenuous on the body. To yield best results schedule dental treatments such as removal of tartar and amalgam as well as fillings, crowns, and dentures. If possible avoid having any teeth pulled.

Blood-purifying and detoxifying herbal infusions and teas are most beneficial.

Consider that the nervous system is more sensitive.

Be cautious with alcohol since the liver is very sensitive.

The stomach could play up and cause gas and heartburn.

If you suffer from rheumatism, don’t air bedding outside, because the damp will remain in the bedding.

Lymphatic therapy is most beneficial.

Body Care During Waning Moon in Cancer ☾

All measures taken to flush out and detoxify are very effective. The closer to New Moon the stronger the impact of the forces.

Apply detoxing facial and body care, treatments of bumps and pimples on the skin, and exfoliating procedures.

Prepare homemade ointments and cosmetics.

Remove body hair; it won't grow back as quickly. Removal of callused skin works best now.

Correction of the nail bed is advisable. Treatment of obstinate athlete’s foot, nail fungus, and warts yields good results.

Massages that serve to relax, ease tension, and detoxify are most effective, such as reflexology massage.

Avoid washing your hair and avoid any haircuts during Cancer days, because hair becomes shaggy and unmanageable.

Enjoy the scents of lilac, lilies of the valley, lilies, and violets.

Garden/Nature During Waning Moon in Cancer ☾

The waning moon in Cancer favors sowing and planting of plants and vegetables that grow below ground, leaf vegetables, and lettuce. Dig over the soil to prepare for planting. Weeding, mowing lawns, and combating pests above ground yields good results.

Water all indoor and outdoor plants. The roots absorb and store more water and as a result will need less frequent watering. Best time to fertilize flowers.

Transplanting, trimming and cutting back plants will favor healthy growth.

Start a compost heap if needed.

This is a planting time with descending forces. Sap is drawn downward, enhancing root formation. Avoid any harvesting, storing and preserving.

Gather herbs for bronchitis, stomach, liver, and gall bladder complaints.

Housework During Waning Moon in Cancer ☾

Housework is dealt with much more successfully, efficiently, and effortlessly during the waning moon. The cleansing effect on nature extends beyond our bodies into the environment. Problem stains are removed readily. Dirt and pollution are best dealt with during waning moon. Any dirt and spots are removed easily in the laundry, in all areas of house cleaning, at the car wash and in dry cleaning. Reduce on cleaners and save money. Support the environment since waste water is broken down much better.

Thoroughly clean wooden and parquet floors, metals, china, etc.

Cleaning, polishing, and waterproofing shoes works best.

Combating mold is more effective.

Because Cancer is linked to the element of water, ventilate rooms briefly and rapidly.

Avoid painting, as paint will take very long to dry.

Nutrition During Waning Moon in Cancer ☾

During waning moon the body is ready to detoxify and cleanse, and weight gain associated with overeating is less likely. Anybody underweight should consider eating larger portions.

All measures taken to flush out and detoxify the sensitive body parts are very effective. The closer to New Moon the stronger the impact of the forces. During the waning moon any cleansing and detox diets will yield the best results. Flush out poisonous substances. Treatment for drug abuse is most effective.

While the moon travels in Cancer, pay attention to the carbohydrates in your diet.

Moodiness may make you want to eat more than is healthy. If you get stomach troubles easily, avoid heavy meals.

Include leafy vegetables in your meals, as the body digests them very well now.

 ♌

3.5. Moon in Leo

Element	Plant Part	Gardening	Sensitive Body Parts	Food Component
Fire – Warm	**Fruit**	**Planting Time**	**Heart, Back, Diaphragm, Circulation, and Arteries**	**Protein**

(Chapter 2.1. features the general description of each zodiac sign.)

Success

When the moon travels in Leo, you will master tasks with more self-confidence and creativity. Determination reigns! We take risks more often, because limits appear to be more easily surmountable.

These are auspicious days for sales, advertising, and publicity.

Watch out in traffic, for some drivers overestimate their abilities.

Leisure Time

Zest for life is in the air. People want to have a fun time, enjoy parties, musical events, movies, etc.

Romance can be very passionate, for Leo represents the element of fire. Possessive feelings can harm a relationship.

These are in general good days for outings; even with cloudy skies the air still feels somewhat warm. But a drying effect will make you more thirsty and dehydrated, so make sure you get plenty to drink.

Watch out for sudden storms, not only in the sky.

☽ Waxing Moon in Leo

Now is the best time to start anything new or alter, reconfigure, and remodel in many areas such as on the job, at school, for leisure, and in the home. It is essential to focus and gather forces, getting plenty of time to rest, recover, regroup, and gain new strength. The closer it is to Full Moon, the stronger the impact of the forces will be.

Health During Waxing Moon in Leo

Healing ointments are easily absorbed. All measures taken to supply nutrient materials and strengthen the sensitive body parts of the heart, back, diaphragm, circulation, arteries are very effective.

Consider that the sense organs are more sensitive as well.

Back and heart problems are more likely to occur.

Avoid overstraining of the heart and cardiovascular system with unusual physical activities.

Expect sleepless nights during these days.

Close to Full Moon any surgery should be avoided if possible, since the healing process slows down and scarring can be more severe.

Body Care During Waxing Moon in Leo

All measures taken to supply nutrient materials and strengthen the body are very effective. Treatments with firming and moisturizing creams are more effective as well as massages to regenerate and strengthen, perhaps added with beneficial massage oils.

Correcting and cutting ingrown nails during these days promotes healthy growth.

If hair is cut during the days the moon travels in Leo, it becomes stronger over time. But be aware that if you get a perm, curls will become quite frizzy. Hair dyes will look more vibrant. Baby's hair is best cut on a Leo day, as it will promote strong and healthy growth.

Enjoy the scents of hibiscus, oleander, and rose.

Garden/Nature During Waxing Moon in Leo

When the moon travels in Leo, any garden work benefiting fruits is most effective. Sow plants and vegetables that grow and flourish above ground, especially fruit and tomatoes. In the appropriate season grafting onto fruit trees is more successful.

 ♌

Also sow and plant vegetables that are highly perishable. Plant trees and bushes. Sow lawns.

Cultivating grains on wet fields is also favorable while the moon is in Leo.

Trim and cut back plants.

Dig over/plow to prepare soil for planting.

Set up a compost heap.

These days are not suitable for fertilizing.

This is a planting time with descending forces. Sap is drawn downward, enhancing root formation. Transplanting yields good results. Harvested produce should be consumed as soon as possible.

In reference to the sensitive body parts, gather herbs for heart and circulation complaints.

Housework During Waxing Moon in Leo ☽

If you intend to remodel or rearrange furniture, start during the waxing moon phase. However, only light housework is advisable, since the waxing moon still requires time to relax, recover, and gather strength.

Every time the moon travels through a star sign that represents the element of fire, it's best to ventilate rooms sufficiently since the air in general is not as humid.

The element of fire makes baking yield good results. Dough for breads, cakes, and cookies rises faster, except on the days close to New Moon. Making cheese is also suitable during these days.

When moon travels in Leo, anything pertaining to fruits is favorable such as preserving and freezing fruits.

Avoid painting during these days.

Nutrition During Waxing Moon in Leo ☽

Everything that is supplied to the body to build up and strengthen is most effective. Stimulants and vitamins have a stronger effect. Any deficiencies of minerals and/or vitamins in the body are best taken care of during the waxing moon. Include all important supplements, tonics, and herbs in your diet. Focus on foods that contain essential minerals and vitamins your body is lacking.

Since the body readily absorbs at this time, you are more likely to gain weight even with a regular amount of food intake. Therefore avoid indulging in rich foods. If you are overweight, eat smaller portions.

Drugs have a much stronger effect. All measures taken to supply nutrient materials and strengthen the sensitive body parts are very effective. Be aware that the body also more readily absorbs poisonous substances. The body retains water more easily, and diuretic measures don't work as effectively.

While the moon travels in Leo, pay attention to proteins in your diet, especially if you don't digest them well during these days.

These are fruit and juice days. Include fruits in your meals, since the body digests them well at this time.

☾ Waning Moon in Leo

Now it's time to be active, detoxify, and remove. If your schedule is flexible, plan your activities during the waning moon phase, because you will reach your goals sooner and more easily, yielding better results.

Health During Waning Moon in Leo ☾

All measures taken to flush out and detoxify the sensitive body parts are very effective. During the waning moon any cleansing and detox diets will yield the best results. Herbal teas, steam room, sauna... anything to detox and cleanse are best utilized between Full Moon and New Moon. The closer to New Moon the stronger the impact of the forces.

The body tends to heal faster during the waning moon and the success rates for surgeries are higher. If you have the choice, schedule surgery, except on the sensitive body parts such as heart, back, diaphragm, and arteries, as well as on the respective body parts of the zodiac sign the sun is in. Scarring is less severe, wounds most likely bleed less than during waxing moon, and surgical operations in general are less strenuous on the body. To yield best results schedule dental treatments such as removal of tartar and amalgam as well as fillings, crowns, and dentures.

Blood-purifying and detoxifying herbal infusions and teas are most beneficial.

Sense organs are more sensitive.

Back and heart problems are more likely to occur.

Avoid over straining of the heart and circulation with unusual physical activities.

Expect sleepless nights during these days.

Body Care During Waning Moon in Leo ☾

All measures taken to flush out and detoxify are very effective. The closer to New Moon the stronger the impact of the forces.

Apply detoxing facial and body care, treatments of bumps and pimples on the skin, and exfoliating procedures.

Prepare homemade ointments and cosmetics.

Remove body hair; it won't grow back as quickly. Removal of callused skin works best now.

Correction of the nail bed is advisable. Treatment of obstinate athlete's foot, nail fungus, and warts yields good results.

Massages that serve to relax, ease tension, and detoxify are most effective, such as reflexology massage.

♌ 

If hair is cut during the days the moon travels in Leo, it becomes stronger over time. But be aware that if you get a perm, curls will become quite frizzy. Hair dyes will look more vibrant. Baby's hair is best cut on a Leo day, as it will promote strong and healthy growth.

Enjoy the scents of hibiscus, oleander, and rose.

Garden/Nature During Waning Moon in Leo ☾

The waning moon favors sowing and planting of plants and vegetables that grow below ground as well as weeding, and pest control.

When the moon travels in Leo, any garden work benefiting fruits is most effective. Therefore sowing and planting fruit and tomatoes, and pruning of fruit trees and bushes yields good results.

Transplanting, trimming and cutting back plants results in healthy growth.

Dig over/plow the soil to prepare for planting.

Set up a compost heap.

These days are not suitable for fertilizing.

This is a planting time with descending forces. Sap is drawn downward, enhancing root formation. Transplanting yields good results. Harvested produce should be consumed as soon as possible.

In reference to the sensitive body parts gather herbs for heart and circulation complaints.

Housework During Waning Moon in Leo ☾

Housework is dealt with much more successfully, efficiently, and effortlessly during the waning moon. The cleansing effect on nature extends beyond our bodies into the environment. Problem stains are removed readily. Dirt and pollution are best dealt with during waning moon. Any dirt and spots are removed easily in the laundry, in all areas of house cleaning, at the car wash and in dry

 ♌

cleaning. Reduce on cleaners and save money. Support the environment since waste water is broken down much better.

Clean and store seasonal clothing now.

Thoroughly clean wooden and parquet floors, metals, china, etc.

Cleaning windows and glass is less likely to produce annoying streaks.

Cleaning, polishing, and waterproofing shoes works best.

Combating mold is more effective.

Every time the moon travels through a star sign that represents the element of fire, it's best to ventilate rooms sufficiently since the air in general is not as humid. Air bedding and mattresses also.

When moon travels in Leo anything pertaining to fruits is favorable, such as preserving and freezing. These days are suitable for making cheese.

Use of more leavening agent is advisable for baking bread, cakes, and cookies.

Avoid painting during these days.

Nutrition During Waning Moon in Leo ☾

The body is ready to detoxify and cleanse, and weight gain associated with overeating is less likely. Anybody underweight should consider eating larger portions.

All measures taken to flush out and detoxify the sensitive body parts are very effective. The closer to New Moon the stronger the impact of the forces. During the waning moon any cleansing and detox diets will yield the best results. Flush out poisonous substances. Treatment for drug abuse is most effective.

While the moon travels in Leo, pay attention to proteins in your diet, especially if you don't digest them well during these days.

These are fruit and juice days. Include fruits in your meals, since the body digests them well at this time.

♍ 

3.6. Moon in Virgo

Element	Plant Part	Gardening	Sensitive Body Parts	Food Component
Earth – Cool	**Root**	**Planting Time**	**Digestive Organs, Nerves, Spleen, and Pancreas**	**Salt**

(Chapter 2.1. features the general description of each zodiac sign.)

Success

Party time is replaced by days for financial and administrative tasks. This is a good time for details, organization, routine, concentration, and duty. Prepare for future success now with realistic and critical assessment.

Leisure Time

This is a good time for health regimes. Improve your health with stretching exercises and yoga. Enjoy a nature walk.

The earth feels cold to the touch, so take slightly warmer clothes.

☽ Waxing Moon in Virgo

Now is the best time to start anything new or alter, reconfigure, and remodel in many areas such as on the job, at school, for leisure, and in the home. It is essential to focus and gather forces, getting plenty of time to rest, recover, regroup, and gain new strength. The closer it is to Full Moon, the stronger the impact of the forces will be.

Health During Waxing Moon in Virgo ☽

Healing ointments are easily absorbed. All measures taken to supply nutrient materials and strengthen the sensitive body parts such as the digestive organs, nerves, spleen, and pancreas are very effective.

Consider that the blood circulation is more sensitive.

Blood-purifying herbal infusions and tea are beneficial now.

 ♍

For a sensitive digestive system, a wholesome diet is recommended.

Dress slightly warmer on these days.

If you have high blood pressure, avoid salty foods.

Massages, lymphatic therapy, and chiropractic treatment to release blockages are beneficial.

Close to Full Moon any surgery should be avoided if possible, since the healing process slows down and scarring can be more severe.

Body Care During Waxing Moon in Virgo ☽

All measures taken to supply nutrient materials and strengthen the body are very effective. Treatments with firming and moisturizing creams are more effective as well as massages to regenerate and strengthen, perhaps added with beneficial massage oils.

Correcting and cutting ingrown nails during these days promotes healthy growth.

Virgo days are best for haircuts because it retains its shape longer.

Perms turn out best and hair dyes will look more vibrant.

Enjoy the scents of lavender, fir, sage, and meadow flowers.

Garden/Nature During Waxing Moon in Virgo ☽

When the moon travels in Virgo, any garden work benefiting roots is most effective. Virgo days are best for sowing and planting, except lettuce. Plant trees which are supposed to grow very tall. Plant hedges and bushes that are meant to grow very fast. Plant and re-pot balcony and indoor plants. Sow lawns.

Transplanting yields good results, trimming and cutting back plants, and planting of cuttings as well.

Start a compost heap if needed.

This is a planting time with descending forces. Sap is drawn downward, enhancing root formation. This is not a suitable time for harvesting and storing.

♍ 

Gather herbs for digestive organs, pancreas, and nervous complaints.

Housework During Waxing Moon in Virgo ☽

If you intend to remodel or rearrange furniture, start during the waxing moon phase. However, only light housework is advisable, since the waxing moon still requires time to relax, recover, and gather strength.

Since Virgo is linked with the element of earth, we easily feel chilly. Therefore air rooms only briefly.

Making pickles, preserves, and cheese yields suboptimal results and should be avoided.

Nutrition During Waxing Moon in Virgo ☽

Everything that is supplied to the body to build up and strengthen is most effective. Stimulants and vitamins have a stronger effect. Any deficiencies of minerals and/or vitamins in the body are best taken care of during the waxing moon. Include all important supplements, tonics, and herbs in your diet. Focus on foods that contain essential minerals and vitamins your body is lacking.

Since the body readily absorbs at this time, you are more likely to gain weight even with a regular amount of food intake. Therefore avoid indulging in rich foods. If you are overweight, eat smaller portions.

Drugs have a much stronger effect. All measures taken to supply nutrient materials and strengthen the sensitive body parts are very effective. Be aware that the body also more readily absorbs poisonous substances. The body retains water more easily, and diuretic measures don't work as effectively.

While the moon travels in Virgo, pay attention to the amount of salt in your diet. Avoid large quantities of salty foods like bacon,

 ♍

ham, salted herring, fatty cheese, and the like. Avoid heavy and greasy foods.

Include root vegetables in your meals, as the body digests them very well now.

☾ Waning Moon in Virgo

Now it's time to be active, detoxify, and remove. If your schedule is flexible, plan your activities during the waning moon phase, because you will reach your goals sooner and more easily, yielding better results.

Health During Waning Moon in Virgo ☾

All measures taken to flush out and detoxify the sensitive body parts are very effective. During the waning moon any cleansing and detox diets will yield the best results. Herbal teas, steam room, sauna... anything to detox and cleanse are best utilized between Full Moon and New Moon. The closer to New Moon the stronger the impact of the forces.

The body tends to heal faster during the waning moon and the success rates for surgeries are higher. If you have the choice, schedule surgery, except on the sensitive body parts such as digestive organs, nerves, spleen, and pancreas, as well as on the respective body parts of the zodiac sign the sun is in. Scarring is less severe, wounds most likely bleed less than during waxing moon, and surgical operations in general are less strenuous on the body. To yield best results schedule dental treatments such as removal of tartar and amalgam as well as fillings, crowns, and dentures.

Blood-purifying and detoxifying herbal infusions and teas are most beneficial.

Consider that the blood circulation is more sensitive.

For a sensitive digestive system, a wholesome diet is recommended.

Dress slightly warmer on these days.

If you have high blood pressure avoid salty foods.

Massages, lymphatic therapy, and chiropractic to release blockages are beneficial.

Body Care During Waning Moon in Virgo ☾

All measures taken to flush out and detoxify are very effective. The closer to New Moon the stronger the impact of the forces.

Apply detoxing facial and body care, treatments of bumps and pimples on the skin, and exfoliating procedures.

Prepare homemade ointments and cosmetics.

Remove body hair; it won't grow back as quickly. Removal of callused skin works best now.

Correction of the nail bed is advisable. Treatment of obstinate athlete's foot, nail fungus, and warts yields good results.

Massages that serve to relax, ease tension, and detoxify are most effective, such as reflexology massage.

Virgo days are best for haircuts because it retains its shape longer.

Perms turn out best.

Enjoy the scents of lavender, fir, sage, and meadow flowers.

Garden/Nature During Waning Moon in Virgo ☾

When the moon travels in Virgo, any garden work benefiting roots is most effective. Virgo days are best for sowing and planting, except lettuce. Plant trees which are supposed to grow very tall. Plant hedges and bushes that are meant to grow very fast. Plant and re-pot balcony and indoor plants.

Dig over the soil to prepare for planting. Transplanting yields good results, trimming and cutting back plants, and planting of cuttings as well.

Weeding and mulching. Start a compost heap if needed.

 ♍

Combat vermin found in the soil. Spread fertilizer and manure. Fertilize flowers with poorly formed roots.

This is a planting time with descending forces. Sap is drawn downward, enhancing root formation. This is not a suitable time for harvesting and storing.

Gather herbs for digestive organs, pancreas, and nervous complaints.

Housework During Waning Moon in Virgo ☾

Housework is dealt with much more successfully, efficiently, and effortlessly during the waning moon. The cleansing effect on nature extends beyond our bodies into the environment. Problem stains are removed readily. Dirt and pollution are best dealt with during waning moon. Any dirt and spots are removed easily in the laundry, in all areas of house cleaning, at the car wash and in dry cleaning. Reduce on cleaners and save money. Support the environment since waste water is broken down much better.

Thoroughly clean wooden and parquet floors, metals, china, etc.

Cleaning, polishing, and waterproofing shoes works best.

Combating mold is more effective.

Since Virgo is linked with the element of earth, we easily feel chilly. Therefore air rooms only briefly.

Making pickles, preserves, and cheese yields suboptimal results and should be avoided.

Good days for painting because the paint dries more quickly and bonds better.

Nutrition During Waning Moon in Virgo ☾

During waning moon the body is ready to detoxify and cleanse, and weight gain associated with overeating is less likely. Anybody underweight should consider eating larger portions.

All measures taken to flush out and detoxify the sensitive body parts are very effective. The closer to New Moon the stronger the impact of the forces. During the waning moon any cleansing and detox diets will yield the best results. Flush out poisonous substances. Treatment for drug abuse is most effective.

While the moon travels in Virgo, pay attention to the amount of salt in your diet. Avoid large quantities of salty foods like bacon, ham, salted herring, fatty cheese, and the like. Avoid heavy and greasy foods.

Include root vegetables in your meals, as the body digests them very well now.

3.7. Moon in Libra

Element	Plant Part	Gardening	Sensitive Body Parts	Food Component
Air – Light	**Flower**	**Planting Time**	**Hips, Kidneys, and Bladder**	**Fat**

(Chapter 2.1. features the general description of each zodiac sign.)

Success

Virgo's more meticulous way of approaching life is replaced by love for beauty in life. The artistic instinct rules, but so, too, does indecisiveness. The forces swing back and forth until equilibrium is achieved.

It's easy to reach compromises with tactful sensitivity.

A sense of judgment will support legal matters.

Leisure Time

Libra's pursuit for harmony and cooperativeness supports good times in romance, friendship, and partnership. Enjoy cultural events. Relax and get pampered with a spa treatment.

Romance can be passionate yet sensitive.

☽ Waxing Moon in Libra

Now is the best time to start anything new or alter, reconfigure, and remodel in many areas such as on the job, at school, for leisure, and in the home. It is essential to focus and gather forces, getting plenty of time to rest, recover, regroup, and gain new strength. The closer it is to Full Moon, the stronger the impact of the forces will be.

Health During Waxing Moon in Libra ☽

Healing ointments are easily absorbed. All measures taken to supply nutrient materials and strengthen the sensitive body parts of the shoulders, arms, hands, and lungs are very effective.

Consider that the glandular system is more sensitive.

If possible avoid having any teeth pulled.

Take special care to keep the area of the bladder and kidneys warm. Apply special exercises for the hip region.

People are more sensitive to light, so bring your sunglasses along when staying outside.

Close to Full Moon any surgery should be avoided if possible, since the healing process slows down and scarring can be more severe.

Body Care During Waxing Moon in Libra ☽

All measures taken to supply nutrient materials and strengthen the body are very effective. Treatments with firming and moisturizing creams are more effective as well as massages to regenerate and strengthen, perhaps added with beneficial massage oils.

Correcting and cutting ingrown nails during these days promotes healthy growth.

Hair dyes will look more vibrant.

Enjoy the scents of roses, violets, and daffodils.

Garden/Nature During Waxing Moon in Libra ☽

When the moon travels in Libra, any garden work benefiting the flower part of a plant is most effective. Sow plants and vegetables that grow and flourish above ground, specially flowers, and medicinal herbs.

Trimming and cutting back plants and transplanting yields good results.

Avoid watering plants, as it attracts pests.

If needed set up a compost heap.

This is a planting time with descending forces. Sap is drawn downward, enhancing root formation. Harvested produce should be consumed as soon as possible.

Gather herbs for kidneys, gall bladder, and hip complaints.

Housework During Waxing Moon in Libra ☽

If you intend to remodel or rearrange furniture, start during the waxing moon phase. However, only light housework is advisable, since the waxing moon still requires time to relax, recover, and gather strength.

Because Libra is linked to the element of air, ventilate rooms thoroughly.

It is a good time for baking cakes and cookies, because the dough rises faster, except on New Moon.

Nutrition During Waxing Moon in Libra ☽

Everything that is supplied to the body to build up and strengthen is most effective. Stimulants and vitamins have a stronger effect. Any deficiencies of minerals and/or vitamins in the body are best taken care of during the waxing moon. Include all important supplements, tonics, and herbs in your diet. Focus on foods that contain essential minerals and vitamins your body is lacking.

Since the body readily absorbs at this time, you are more likely to gain weight even with a regular amount of food intake. Therefore avoid indulging in rich foods. If you are overweight, eat smaller portions.

Drugs have a much stronger effect. All measures taken to supply nutrient materials and strengthen the sensitive body parts are very effective. Be aware that the body also more readily absorbs poisonous substances. The body retains water more easily, and diuretic measures don't work as effectively.

While the moon travels in Libra, pay attention to the fats in your diet and to any particularly tempting foods today. Most likely the "wrong" things taste best.

If you have high cholesterol eat a low fat diet.

Include flower vegetables in your meals, as the body digests them very well now.

☾ Waning Moon in Libra

Now it's time to be active, detoxify, and remove. If your schedule is flexible, plan your activities during the waning moon phase, because you will reach your goals sooner and more easily, yielding better results.

Health During Waning Moon in Libra ☾

All measures taken to flush out and detoxify the sensitive body parts are very effective. During the waning moon any cleansing and detox diets will yield the best results. Herbal teas, steam room, sauna... anything to detox and cleanse are best utilized between Full Moon and New Moon. The closer to New Moon the stronger the impact of the forces.

The body tends to heal faster during the waning moon and the success rates for surgeries are higher. If you have the choice, schedule surgery, except on the sensitive body parts such as hips, kidneys, and bladder, as well as on the respective body parts of the zodiac sign the sun is in. Scarring is less severe, wounds most likely bleed less than during waxing moon, and surgical operations in general are less strenuous on the body. To yield best results schedule dental treatments such as removal of tartar and amalgam as well as fillings, crowns, and dentures. Avoid treatment of periodontitis and gums and also if possible avoid having any teeth pulled.

Blood-purifying and detoxifying herbal infusions and teas are most beneficial.

Consider that the glandular system is more sensitive.

Take special care to keep the area of the bladder and kidneys warm. Apply special exercises for the hip region.

People are more sensitive to light, so bring your sunglasses along when staying outside.

Body Care During Waning Moon in Libra ☾

All measures taken to flush out and detoxify are very effective. The closer to New Moon the stronger the impact of the forces.

Apply detoxing facial and body care, treatments of bumps and pimples on the skin, and exfoliating procedures.

Prepare homemade ointments and cosmetics.

Remove body hair; it won't grow back as quickly. Removal of callused skin works best now.

Correction of the nail bed is advisable. Treatment of obstinate athlete's foot, nail fungus, and warts yields good results.

Massages that serve to relax, ease tension, and detoxify are most effective, such as reflexology massage.

Enjoy the scents of roses, violets, and daffodils.

Garden/Nature During Waning Moon in Libra ☾

The waning moon in Libra favors sowing and planting of plants and vegetables that grow below ground as well as weeding and pest control.

Dig over/plow the soil to prepare for planting. If needed set up a compost heap.

Transplanting, trimming and cutting back plants will favor healthy growth.

Avoid watering plants, as it attracts pests.

Fertilize flowers that no longer bloom.

This is a planting time with descending forces. Sap is drawn downward, enhancing root formation. Harvested produce should be consumed as soon as possible.

Gather herbs for kidneys, gall bladder, and hip complaints.

Housework During Waning Moon in Libra ☾

Housework is dealt with much more successfully, efficiently, and effortlessly during the waning moon. The cleansing effect on nature extends beyond our bodies into the environment. Problem stains are removed readily. Dirt and pollution are best dealt with during waning moon. Any dirt and spots are removed easily in the laundry, in all areas of house cleaning, at the car wash and in dry cleaning. Reduce on cleaners and save money. Support the environment since waste water is broken down much better.

Clean and store seasonal clothing now.

Thoroughly clean wooden and parquet floors, metals, china, etc.

Cleaning windows and glass is less likely to produce annoying streaks.

Cleaning, polishing, and waterproofing shoes works best.

Because Libra is linked to the element of air, ventilate rooms thoroughly.

Making preserves yields good results.

Good time for baking bread, cakes, and cookies, if more leavening agent is added to the dough.

Nutrition During Waning Moon in Libra ☾

During waning moon the body is ready to detoxify and cleanse, and weight gain associated with overeating is less likely. Anybody underweight should consider eating larger portions.

All measures taken to flush out and detoxify the sensitive body parts are very effective. The closer to New Moon the stronger the

impact of the forces. During the waning moon any cleansing and detox diets will yield the best results. Flush out poisonous substances. Treatment for drug abuse is most effective.

While the moon travels in Libra, pay attention to the fats in your diet and to any particularly tempting foods today. Most likely the "wrong" things taste best.

If you have high cholesterol eat a low fat diet.

Include flower vegetables in your meals, as the body digests them very well now.

3.8. Moon in Scorpio

Element	Plant Part	Gardening	Sensitive Body Parts	Food Component
Water – Wetness	**Leaf**	**Planting Time**	**Sex Organs and Ureter**	**Carbohydrate**

(Chapter 2.1. features the general description of each zodiac sign.)

Success

Attachment to passionate quarrels and problems can influence our tasks during Scorpio days. Critical and superstitious behavior emerges, especially pertaining to money. A penetrating power will strengthen your capacity to act, but it can turn into bossy aggressiveness and attachment to conflicts.

An increased perception opens our interest for the essentials and helps to discover hidden potentials.

Leisure Time

Feelings of loyalty and the pursuit of idealism come into prominence. You may want to relax within your close family, with meditation and relaxation exercises. A longing to feel safe will be nurtured if you focus on habits and rituals.

An increased sensitivity will help you enjoy every moment.

Romance can be very passionate. Deep feelings will prevail.

If you plan outdoor excursions, consider an increased possibility of showers.

☽ Waxing Moon in Scorpio

Now is the best time to start anything new or alter, reconfigure, and remodel in many areas such as on the job, at school, for leisure, and in the home. It is essential to focus and gather forces, getting plenty of time to rest, recover, regroup, and gain new strength. The closer it is to Full Moon, the stronger the impact of the forces will be.

Health During Waxing Moon in Scorpio ☽

Healing ointments are easily absorbed. All measures taken to supply nutrient materials and strengthen the sensitive body parts of the sex organs and ureter are very effective.

Consider that the nervous system is more sensitive.

If you are susceptible to female disorders, as a preventative measure apply hip baths using yarrow.

Pregnant women should avoid any exertion because miscarriages are more likely.

Keep region of the pelvis, kidneys, and feet warm to prevent infection of the bladder and kidneys.

Lymphatic therapy is most beneficial.

Close to Full Moon any surgery should be avoided if possible, since the healing process slows down and scarring can be more severe.

Body Care During Waxing Moon in Scorpio ☽

All measures taken to supply nutrient materials and strengthen the body are very effective. Treatments with firming and moisturizing creams are more effective as well as massages that serve to regenerate, and strengthen, perhaps with the aid of appropriate oils.

Hair dyes applied now, will look more vibrant.

Enjoy the scents of anemone, cornflower, oregano, and thuja.

Garden/Nature During Waxing Moon in Scorpio ☽

When the moon travels in Scorpio, any garden work benefiting the leaves of a plant is most effective. Sow plants and vegetables that grow and flourish above ground, any leaf vegetables, but no lettuce.

Scorpio days are good for sowing, planting, harvesting and drying every kind of medicinal herbs.

Transplanting yields good results. Combat slugs and snails.

Water all indoor and outdoor plants. The roots absorb and store more water and as a result will need less frequent watering.

Trimming, cutting back plants, and mowing lawns will result in healthy growth. But avoid pruning fruit trees and bushes as well as cutting down any trees.

If needed, set up a compost heap.

This is a planting time with descending forces. Sap is drawn downward, enhancing root formation. Harvested produce should be consumed as soon as possible.

Housework During Waxing Moon in Scorpio ☽

If you intend to remodel or rearrange furniture, start during the waxing moon phase. However, only light housework is advisable, since the waxing moon still requires time to relax, recover, and gather strength.

Because Scorpio is linked to the element of water, ventilate rooms briefly and rapidly. Don't air any mattresses.

Any dirt and spots are easily removed in the laundry.

Avoid painting, as paint will take very long to dry.

Nutrition During Waxing Moon in Scorpio ☽

Everything that is supplied to the body to build up and strengthen is most effective. Stimulants and vitamins have a stronger effect. Any deficiencies of minerals and/or vitamins in the body are best taken care of during the waxing moon. Include all important supplements, tonics, and herbs in your diet. Focus on foods that contain essential minerals and vitamins your body is lacking.

Since the body readily absorbs at this time, you are more likely to gain weight even with a regular amount of food intake. Therefore avoid indulging in rich foods. If you are overweight, eat smaller portions.

Drugs have a much stronger effect. All measures taken to supply nutrient materials and strengthen the sensitive body parts are very effective. Be aware that the body also more readily absorbs poisonous substances. The body retains water more easily, and diuretic measures don't work as effectively.

While the moon travels in Scorpio, pay attention to the carbohydrates in your diet.

Include leafy vegetables in your meals, as the body digests them very well now.

☾ Waning Moon in Scorpio

Now it's time to be active, detoxify, and remove. If your schedule is flexible, plan your activities during the waning moon phase, because you will reach your goals sooner and more easily, yielding better results.

Health During Waning Moon in Scorpio ☾

All measures taken to flush out and detoxify the sensitive body parts are very effective. During the waning moon any cleansing and detox diets will yield the best results. Herbal teas, steam room, sauna... anything to detox and cleanse are best utilized between Full Moon and New Moon. The closer to New Moon the stronger the impact of the forces.

The body tends to heal faster during the waning moon and the success rates for surgeries are higher. If you have the choice, schedule surgery, except on the sensitive body parts such as sex organs and ureter, as well as on the respective body parts of the zodiac sign the sun is in. Scarring is less severe, wounds most likely bleed less than during waxing moon, and surgical operations in general are less

strenuous on the body. To yield best results schedule dental treatments such as removal of tartar and amalgam as well as fillings, crowns, and dentures.

Blood-purifying and detoxifying herbal infusions and teas are most beneficial.

Consider that the nervous system is more sensitive.

If you are susceptible to female disorders, as a preventative measure apply hip baths using yarrow.

Pregnant women should avoid any exertion because miscarriages are more likely.

Keep region of the pelvis, kidneys, and feet warm to prevent infection of the bladder and kidneys.

Lymphatic therapy is most beneficial.

Body Care During Waning Moon in Scorpio ☾

All measures taken to flush out and detoxify are very effective. The closer to New Moon the stronger the impact of the forces.

Apply detoxing facial and body care, treatments of bumps and pimples on the skin, and exfoliating procedures.

Prepare homemade ointments and cosmetics.

Remove body hair; it won't grow back as quickly. Removal of callused skin works best now.

Correction of the nail bed is advisable. Treatment of obstinate athlete's foot, nail fungus, and warts yields good results.

Massages that serve to relax, ease tension, and detoxify are most effective, such as reflexology massage.

Enjoy the scents of anemone, cornflower, oregano, and thuja.

Garden/Nature During Waning Moon in Scorpio ☾

The waning moon in Scorpio favors sowing and planting of plants

and vegetables that grow below ground, leaf vegetables, and lettuce. Dig over the soil to prepare for planting. Weeding, mowing lawns, and combating pests yields good results. Scorpio days are good for sowing, planting, harvesting and drying every kind of medicinal herbs.

Water all indoor and outdoor plants, the roots absorb and store more water and as a result need less frequent watering. Best time to fertilize flowers and meadows, but no vegetables.

Transplanting, trimming and cutting back plants will favor healthy growth. Avoid cutting down trees, because bark beetles could settle in easily.

Start a compost heap if needed.

This is a planting time with descending forces. Sap is drawn downward, enhancing root formation. Harvested produce should be consumed as soon as possible.

Housework During Waning Moon in Scorpio ☾

Housework is dealt with much more successfully, efficiently, and effortlessly during the waning moon. The cleansing effect on nature extends beyond our bodies into the environment. Problem stains are removed readily. Dirt and pollution are best dealt with during waning moon. Any dirt and spots are removed easily in the laundry, in all areas of house cleaning, at the car wash and in dry cleaning. Reduce on cleaners and save money. Support the environment since waste water is broken down much better.

Thoroughly clean wooden and parquet floors, metals, china, etc.

Cleaning, polishing, and waterproofing shoes works best.

Combating mold is more effective.

Because Scorpio is linked to the element of water, ventilate rooms briefly and rapidly.

Avoid painting, as paint will take very long to dry.

Nutrition During Waning Moon in Scorpio ☾

During waning moon body is ready to detoxify and cleanse, and weight gain associated with overeating is less likely. Anybody underweight should consider eating larger portions.

All measures taken to flush out and detoxify the sensitive body parts are very effective. The closer to New Moon the stronger the impact of the forces. During the waning moon any cleansing and detox diets will yield the best results. Flush out poisonous substances. Treatment for drug abuse is most effective.

While the moon travels in Scorpio, pay attention to the carbohydrates in your diet.

Include leafy vegetables in your meals, as the body digests them very well now.

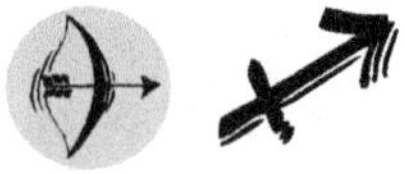

3.9. Moon in Sagittarius

Element	Plant Part	Gardening	Sensitive Body Parts	Food Component
Fire – Warm	**Fruit**	**Turning Point**	**Thighs and Veins**	**Protein**

(Chapter 2.1. features the general description of each zodiac sign.)

Success

Inquisitiveness and exuberant inspiration lead to new horizons. Insight and love for truth reign.

Bringing together is more important than splitting asunder.

Expansive forces will assist in legal matters, discussions, and debates.

Watch out in traffic for reckless drivers.

Leisure Time

Expansion feels great, and travel, short trips, and outings are most welcome. A competitive spirit excites any sports event.

Talk things out when necessary. Romance can be very passionate, for Sagittarius represents the element of fire.

These are in general good days for outings, for even with cloudy skies the air still feels somewhat warm. But a drying effect will make you more thirsty and dehydrated, so make sure you get plenty to drink.

Waxing Moon in Sagittarius

Now is the best time to start anything new or alter, reconfigure, and remodel in many areas such as on the job, at school, for leisure, and in the home. It is essential to focus and gather forces, getting plenty of time to rest, recover, regroup, and gain new strength. The closer it is to Full Moon, the stronger the impact of the forces will be.

Health During Waxing Moon in Sagittarius ☽

Healing ointments are easily absorbed. All measures taken to supply nutrient materials and strengthen the sensitive body parts of the thighs and veins are very effective.

Consider that the sense organs are more sensitive as well.

Pains often arise in the sciatic nerve, veins, the small of the back, and thighs.

Avoid overstraining the body with unusual physical activities.

Close to Full Moon any surgery should be avoided if possible, since the healing process slows down and scarring can be more severe.

Body Care During Waxing Moon in Sagittarius ☽

All measures taken to supply nutrient materials and strengthen the body are very effective. Treatments with firming and moisturizing creams are more effective as well as massages to regenerate and strengthen, perhaps added with beneficial massage oils.

Correcting and cutting ingrown nails during these days promotes healthy growth.

Hair dyes will look more vibrant.

Enjoy the scents of calendula (marigold), geranium, and rosemary.

Garden/Nature During Waxing Moon in Sagittarius ☽

When the moon travels in Sagittarius, any garden work benefiting fruits is most effective. Sow plants and vegetables that grow and flourish above ground, that grow tall, especially tomatoes, but no lettuce. In the appropriate season grafting onto fruit trees is more successful.

Cultivating grains, particularly corn, is also favorable while the moon is in Sagittarius.

Transplanting yields good results.

This is a turning point. Whether transitioning from ascending to descending forces or vice versa, both forces are at work and neutralize each other. As a result, neither harvesting nor planting yields best results.

Gather herbs for vein diseases.

Housework During Waxing Moon in Sagittarius ☽

If you intend to remodel or rearrange furniture, start during the waxing moon phase. However, only light housework is advisable, since the waxing moon still requires time to relax, recover, and gather strength.

Every time the moon travels through a star sign that represents the element of fire, it's best to ventilate rooms sufficiently since the air in general is not as humid.

The element of fire makes baking yield good results. Dough for breads, cakes, and cookies rises faster, except on the days close to New Moon. Making cheese is also suitable during these days.

Nutrition During Waxing Moon in Sagittarius ☽

Everything that is supplied to the body to build up and strengthen is most effective. Stimulants and vitamins have a stronger effect. Any deficiencies of minerals and/or vitamins in the body are best taken care of during the waxing moon. Include all important supplements, tonics, and herbs in your diet. Focus on foods that contain essential minerals and vitamins your body is lacking.

Since the body readily absorbs at this time, you are more likely to gain weight even with a regular amount of food intake. Therefore avoid indulging in rich foods. If you are overweight, eat smaller portions.

Drugs have a much stronger effect. All measures taken to supply nutrient materials and strengthen the sensitive body parts are very effective. Be aware that the body also more readily absorbs poisonous substances. The body retains water more easily, and diuretic measures don't work as effectively.

While the moon travels in Sagittarius pay attention to proteins in your diet, especially if you don't digest them well during these days.

These are fruit and juice days. Include fruits in your meals, since the body digests them well at this time.

☾ Waning Moon in Sagittarius

Now it's time to be active, detoxify, and remove. If your schedule is flexible, plan your activities during the waning moon phase, because you will reach your goals sooner and more easily, yielding better results.

Health During Waning Moon in Sagittarius ☾

All measures taken to flush out and detoxify the sensitive body parts are very effective. During the waning moon any cleansing and detox diets will yield the best results. Herbal teas, steam room, sauna... anything to detox and cleanse are best utilized between Full Moon and New Moon. The closer to New Moon the stronger the impact of the forces.

The body tends to heal faster during the waning moon and the success rates for surgeries are higher. If you have the choice, schedule surgery, except on the sensitive body parts such as thighs and veins, as well as on the respective body parts of the zodiac sign the sun is in. Scarring is less severe, wounds most likely bleed less than during waxing moon, and surgical operations in general are less strenuous on the body. To yield best results schedule dental treatments such as removal of tartar and amalgam as well as fillings, crowns, and dentures.

Blood-purifying and detoxifying herbal infusions and teas are most beneficial.

Sense organs are more sensitive.

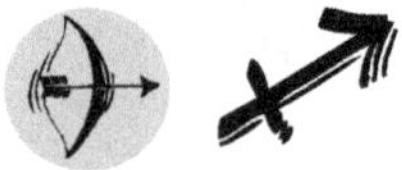

Pains often arise in the sciatic nerve, veins, the small of the back, and thighs.

Avoid overstraining the body with unusual physical activities.

Body Care During Waning Moon in Sagittarius ☾

All measures taken to flush out and detoxify are very effective. The closer to New Moon the stronger the impact of the forces.

Apply detoxing facial and body care, treatments of bumps and pimples on the skin, and exfoliating procedures.

Prepare homemade ointments and cosmetics.

Remove body hair; it won't grow back as quickly. Removal of callused skin works best now.

Correction of the nail bed is advisable. Treatment of obstinate athlete's foot, nail fungus, and warts yields good results.

Massages that serve to relax, ease tension, and detoxify are most effective, such as reflexology massage.

Enjoy the scents of calendula (marigold), geranium, and rosemary.

Garden/Nature During Waning Moon in Sagittarius ☾

The waning moon favors sowing and planting of plants and vegetables that grow below ground as well as weeding, and combating pests above ground.

The moon traveling in Sagittarius affects the fruit part of plants. Therefore pruning of fruit trees and bushes yields good results.

Trimming and cutting back plants results in healthy growth.

Fertilize grains, vegetables, and fruit.

Set up a compost heap.

Dig over/plow the soil to prepare for planting.

Cultivating grains, particularly corn, is also favorable while the moon is in Sagittarius.

♐ 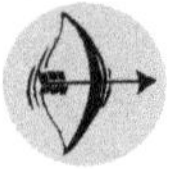

This is a turning point. Whether transitioning from ascending to descending forces or vice versa, both forces are at work and neutralize each other. As a result, neither harvesting nor planting yields best results.

Gather herbs for vein diseases.

Housework During Waning Moon in Sagittarius ☾

Housework is dealt with much more successfully, efficiently, and effortlessly during the waning moon. The cleansing effect on nature extends beyond our bodies into the environment. Problem stains are removed readily. Dirt and pollution are best dealt with during waning moon. Any dirt and spots are removed easily in the laundry, in all areas of house cleaning, at the car wash and in dry cleaning. Reduce on cleaners and save money. Support the environment since waste water is broken down much better.

Thoroughly clean wooden and parquet floors, metals, china, etc.

Cleaning windows and glass is less likely to produce annoying streaks.

Cleaning, polishing, and waterproofing shoes works best.

Combating mold is more effective.

Every time the moon travels through a star sign that represents the element of fire, it's best to ventilate rooms sufficiently since the air in general is not as humid. Air bedding and mattresses also.

When moon travels in Leo anything pertaining to fruits is favorable, such as preserving and freezing. These days are suitable for making cheese.

Use of more leavening agent is advisable for baking bread, cakes, and cookies.

Good days for painting because the paint dries quicker and bonds better.

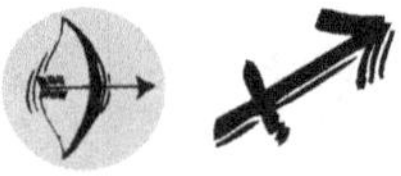

Nutrition During Waning Moon in Sagittarius ☾

The body is ready to detoxify and cleanse, and weight gain associated with overeating is less likely. Anybody underweight should consider eating larger portions.

All measures taken to flush out and detoxify the sensitive body parts are very effective. The closer to New Moon the stronger the impact of the forces. During the waning moon any cleansing and detox diets will yield the best results. Flush out poisonous substances. Treatment for drug abuse is most effective.

While the moon travels in Sagittarius pay attention to proteins in your diet, especially if you don't digest them well during these days.

These are fruit and juice days. Include fruits in your meals, since the body digests them well at this time.

3.10. Moon in Capricorn

Element	Plant Part	Gardening	Sensitive Body Parts	Food Component
Earth – Cool	Root	Harvest Time	Knees, Bones, Joints, and Skin	Salt

(Chapter 2.1. features the general description of each zodiac sign.)

Success

Career and business are in the foreground now and thinking becomes clear and serious, but somewhat inflexible. Perseverance and reasoning assist in financial matters, planning, and contracts. The values of tradition, authority, and discipline impact our endeavors.

Leisure Time

Money is not likely to be wasted in a shopping spree. Many are drawn to enjoy cultural events. The earth feels cold to the touch, so take slightly warmer clothes.

☽ Waxing Moon in Capricorn

Now is the best time to start anything new or alter, reconfigure, and remodel in many areas such as on the job, at school, for leisure, and in the home. It is essential to focus and gather forces, getting plenty of time to rest, recover, regroup, and gain new strength. The closer it is to Full Moon, the stronger the impact of the forces will be.

Health During Waxing Moon in Capricorn ☽

Healing ointments are easily absorbed. All measures taken to supply nutrient materials and strengthen the sensitive body parts of the knees, bones, joints, and skin are very effective.

Consider that the blood circulation is more sensitive.

Avoid overstraining bones and knees, and apply gentle stretching exercises only. If you have any meniscus problems, it is especially important to not overstrain.

Therapy for skin diseases is highly effective.

Dress slightly warmer on these days.

If you have high blood pressure avoid salty foods.

Massages, lymphatic therapy, and chiropractic treatment to release blockages are beneficial.

Close to Full Moon any surgery should be avoided if possible, since the healing process slows down and scarring can be more severe.

Body Care During Waxing Moon in Capricorn ☽

All measures taken to supply nutrient materials and strengthen the body are very effective. Treatments with firming and moisturizing creams are more effective as well as massages to regenerate and strengthen, perhaps added with beneficial massage oils.

Correcting and cutting ingrown nails during these days promotes healthy growth.

While the moon travels in Capricorn, every kind of skin care is beneficial.

Cutting and filing toenails and fingernails on days of Capricorn will make the nails grow stronger over time.

Hair dyes will look more vibrant.

Enjoy the scents of cedar and juniper.

Garden/Nature During Waxing Moon in Capricorn ☽

When the moon travels in Capricorn, any garden work benefiting roots is most effective. Sow plants, herbs, and vegetables that grow and flourish above ground.

Transplanting yields good results.

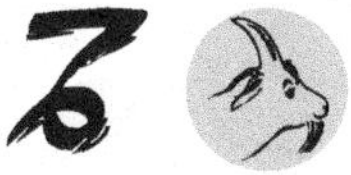

This is harvest time with ascending forces! Sap is rising, enhancing plant growth above ground, and fruits and vegetables are at their most juicy. Harvest produce is suitable for storage. Harvest root vegetables.

Gather herbs for bone, joint, and skin diseases.

Housework During Waxing Moon in Capricorn ☽

If you intend to remodel or rearrange furniture, start during the waxing moon phase. However, only light housework is advisable, since the waxing moon still requires time to relax, recover, and gather strength.

Because Capricorn is linked to the element of earth, we easily feel chilly. Therefore air rooms only briefly.

Preserving root vegetables yields good results.

Avoid dry cleaning when the moon travels in Capricorn, as the fabric may develop unwanted glossy blotches.

Nutrition During Waxing Moon in Capricorn ☽

Everything that is supplied to the body to build up and strengthen is most effective. Stimulants and vitamins have a stronger effect. Any deficiencies of minerals and/or vitamins in the body are best taken care of during the waxing moon. Include all important supplements, tonics, and herbs in your diet. Focus on foods that contain essential minerals and vitamins your body is lacking.

Since the body readily absorbs at this time, you are more likely to gain weight even with a regular amount of food intake. Therefore avoid indulging in rich foods. If you are overweight, eat smaller portions.

Drugs have a much stronger effect. All measures taken to supply nutrient materials and strengthen the sensitive body parts are very effective. Be aware that the body also more readily absorbs poisonous substances. The body retains water more easily, and diuretic measures don't work as effectively.

While the moon travels in Capricorn, pay attention to the amount of salt in your diet. Avoid large quantities of salty foods like bacon, ham, salted herring, fatty cheese, and the like. Avoid heavy and greasy foods.

Include root vegetables in your meals, as the body digests them very well now.

☾ Waning Moon in Capricorn

Now it's time to be active, detoxify, and remove. If your schedule is flexible, plan your activities during the waning moon phase, because you will reach your goals sooner and more easily, yielding better results.

Health During Waning Moon in Capricorn ☾

All measures taken to flush out and detoxify the sensitive body parts are very effective. During the waning moon any cleansing and detox diets will yield the best results. Herbal teas, steam room, sauna... anything to detox and cleanse are best utilized between Full Moon and New Moon. The closer to New Moon the stronger the impact of the forces.

The body tends to heal faster during the waning moon and the success rates for surgeries are higher. If you have the choice, schedule surgery, except on the sensitive body parts such as knees, joints, bones, and skin, as well as on the respective body parts of the zodiac sign the sun is in. Scarring is less severe, wounds most likely bleed less than during waxing moon, and surgical operations in general are less strenuous on the body. To yield best results schedule dental treatments such as removal of tartar and amalgam as well as fillings, crowns, and dentures.

Blood-purifying and detoxifying herbal infusions and teas are most beneficial.

Consider that the blood circulation is more sensitive.

Avoid overstraining bones and knees, and apply gentle stretching exercises only. If you have any meniscus problems, it is especially important to not overstrain.

Dress slightly warmer on these days.

If you have high blood pressure avoid salty foods.

Massages, lymphatic therapy, and chiropractic to release blockages are beneficial.

Body Care During Waning Moon in Capricorn ☾

All measures taken to flush out and detoxify are very effective. The closer to New Moon the stronger the impact of the forces.

Apply detoxing facial and body care, treatments of bumps and pimples on the skin, and exfoliating procedures.

Prepare homemade ointments and cosmetics.

Remove body hair, it may not grow back.

Correction of the nail bed is advisable. Treatment of obstinate athlete's foot, nail fungus, and warts yields good results.

Massages that serve to relax, ease tension, and detoxify are most effective, such as reflexology massage.

Cutting and filing toenails and fingernails on days of Capricorn will make the nails grow stronger over time.

Enjoy the scents of cedar and juniper.

Garden/Nature During Waning Moon in Capricorn ☾

When the moon travels in Capricorn any garden work benefiting roots is most effective. Sow and plant root vegetables and winter vegetables according to season.

Dig over the soil to prepare for planting. Weeding, harrowing weeds, and mulching is recommended. Start a compost heap if needed.

 ♑

Trimming and cutting back plants results in healthy growth as well as plant cuttings. Clear and thin out plants, forest edges, and hedges.

Spread fertilizer and manure. Fertilize flowers with poorly formed roots.

Combat vermin.

This is harvest time with ascending forces! Sap is rising, enhancing plant growth above ground, and fruits and vegetables are at their most juicy. Harvest produce is suitable for storage. Harvest root vegetables.

Gather herbs for bone, joint, and skin diseases.

Housework During Waning Moon in Capricorn ☾

Housework is dealt with much more successfully, efficiently, and effortlessly during the waning moon. The cleansing effect on nature extends beyond our bodies into the environment. Problem stains are removed readily. Dirt and pollution are best dealt with during waning moon. Any dirt and spots are removed easily in the laundry, in all areas of house cleaning, at the car wash and in dry cleaning. Reduce on cleaners and save money. Support the environment since waste water is broken down much better.

Avoid dry cleaning when the moon travels in Capricorn, as the fabric may develop unwanted glossy blotches.

Thoroughly clean wooden and parquet floors, metals, china, etc.

Cleaning, polishing, and waterproofing shoes works best.

Combating mold is more effective.

Because Capricorn is linked to the element of earth, we easily feel chilly. Therefore air rooms only briefly.

Preserving root vegetables yields good results. Slice cabbage now to ferment into sauerkraut.

Good days for painting because the paint dries more quickly and bonds better.

Nutrition During Waning Moon in Capricorn ☾

During waning moon the body is ready to detoxify and cleanse, and weight gain associated with overeating is less likely. Anybody underweight should consider eating larger portions.

All measures taken to flush out and detoxify the sensitive body parts are very effective. The closer to New Moon the stronger the impact of the forces. During the waning moon any cleansing and detox diets will yield the best results. Flush out poisonous substances. Treatment for drug abuse is most effective.

While the moon travels in Capricorn, pay attention to the amount of salt in your diet. Avoid large quantities of salty foods like bacon, ham, salted herring, fatty cheese, and the like. Avoid heavy and greasy foods.

Include root vegetables in your meals, as the body digests them very well now.

3.11. Moon in Aquarius

Element	Plant Part	Gardening	Sensitive Body Parts	Food Component
Air – Light	**Flower**	**Harvest Time**	**Lower Legs and Veins**	**Fat**

(Chapter 2.1. features the general description of each zodiac sign.)

Success

After the structure and discipline of Capricorn come the qualities of inspiration, optimism, and impatience. Rational thinking, creativity and imagination spark new ideas and inspire planning for the future. Shying away from any routine tasks people will feel more drawn to anything new. Instead of gridlocked structures choose new possibilities.

Creativity and imagination assist in advertising.

Leisure Time

Inspiration and optimism will boost friendship, social gatherings, and parties. You will feel drawn to areas where you can express your creativity and imagination and dwell in dreams and utopian ideas. It is easier now to perceive intuitive thoughts.

☽ Waxing Moon in Aquarius

Now is the best time to start anything new or alter, reconfigure, and remodel in many areas such as on the job, at school, for leisure, and in the home. It is essential to focus and gather forces, getting plenty of time to rest, recover, regroup, and gain new strength. The closer it is to Full Moon, the stronger the impact of the forces will be.

Health During Waxing Moon in Aquarius ☽

Healing ointments are easily absorbed. All measures taken to supply nutrient materials and strengthen the sensitive body parts of the lower legs and veins are very effective.

Consider that the glandular system is more sensitive.

If possible avoid having any teeth pulled.

Avoid inflammation of the veins. Apply ointments to lower legs, and rest legs in a raised position. If you suffer from varicose veins avoid long periods of standing.

While exercising go easy on the ankles.

People are more sensitive to light, so bring your sunglasses along when staying outside.

Close to Full Moon any surgery should be avoided if possible, since the healing process slows down and scarring can be more severe.

Body Care During Waxing Moon in Aquarius ☽

All measures taken to supply nutrient materials and strengthen the body are very effective. Treatments with firming and moisturizing creams are more effective as well as massages to regenerate and strengthen, perhaps added with beneficial massage oils.

Correcting and cutting ingrown nails during these days promotes healthy growth.

Hair dyes will look more vibrant.

Enjoy the scents of cyclamen, peach, and wild roses.

Garden/Nature During Waxing Moon in Aquarius ☽

When the moon travels in Aquarius, any garden work benefiting the flower part of a plant is most effective.

Avoid watering plants, as it attracts pests.

This is harvest time with ascending forces! Sap is rising, enhancing plant growth above ground, and fruits and vegetables are at their most juicy. Harvest produce is especially suitable for storage.

Gather herbs for vein diseases.

Housework During Waxing Moon in Aquarius ☽

If you intend to remodel or rearrange furniture, start during the waxing moon phase. However, only light housework is advisable, since the waxing moon still requires time to relax, recover, and gather strength.

Because Aquarius is linked to the element of air, ventilate rooms thoroughly.

It is a good time for baking cakes and cookies, because the dough rises faster, except on New Moon.

Making preserves yields good results.

Nutrition During Waxing Moon in Aquarius ☽

Everything that is supplied to the body to build up and strengthen is most effective. Stimulants and vitamins have a stronger effect. Any deficiencies of minerals and/or vitamins in the body are best taken care of during the waxing moon. Include all important supplements, tonics, and herbs in your diet. Focus on foods that contain essential minerals and vitamins your body is lacking.

Since the body readily absorbs at this time, you are more likely to gain weight even with a regular amount of food intake. Therefore avoid indulging in rich foods. If you are overweight, eat smaller portions.

Drugs have a much stronger effect. All measures taken to supply nutrient materials and strengthen the sensitive body parts are very effective. Be aware that the body also more readily absorbs poisonous substances. The body retains water more easily, and diuretic measures don't work as effectively.

While the moon travels in Aquarius, pay attention to the fats in your diet and to any particularly tempting foods today. Most likely the "wrong" things taste best.

If you have high cholesterol eat a low fat diet.

Include flower vegetables in your meals, as the body digests them very well now.

☾ Waning Moon in Aquarius

Now it's time to be active, detoxify, and remove. If your schedule is flexible, plan your activities during the waning moon phase, because you will reach your goals sooner and more easily, yielding better results.

Health During Waning Moon in Aquarius ☾

All measures taken to flush out and detoxify the sensitive body parts are very effective. During the waning moon any cleansing and detox diets will yield the best results. Herbal teas, steam room, sauna... anything to detox and cleanse are best utilized between Full Moon and New Moon. The closer to New Moon the stronger the impact of the forces.

The body tends to heal faster during the waning moon and the success rates for surgeries are higher. If you have the choice, schedule surgery, except on the sensitive body parts such as lower legs, and veins, as well as on the respective body parts of the zodiac sign the sun is in. Scarring is less severe, wounds most likely bleed less than during waxing moon, and surgical operations in general are less strenuous on the body. To yield best results schedule dental treatments such as removal of tartar and amalgam as well as fillings, crowns, and dentures.

Blood-purifying and detoxifying herbal infusions and teas are most beneficial.

Consider that the glandular system is more sensitive.

Avoid inflammation of the veins. Apply ointments to lower legs, and rest legs in a raised position. If you suffer from varicose veins avoid long periods of standing.

While exercising go easy on the ankles.

People are more sensitive to light, so bring your sunglasses along when staying outside.

Body Care During Waning Moon in Aquarius ☾

All measures taken to flush out and detoxify are very effective. The closer to New Moon the stronger the impact of the forces.

Apply detoxing facial and body care, treatments of bumps and pimples on the skin, and exfoliating procedures.

Prepare homemade ointments and cosmetics.

Remove body hair; it won't grow back as quickly. Removal of callused skin works best now.

Correction of the nail bed is advisable. Treatment of obstinate athlete's foot, nail fungus, and warts yields good results.

Massages that serve to relax, ease tension, and detoxify are most effective, such as reflexology massage.

Enjoy the scents of cyclamen, peach, and wild roses.

Garden/Nature During Waning Moon in Aquarius ☾

The waning moon in Aquarius favors trimming and cutting back plants as well as pest control. Dig over/plow to prepare soil for planting. If needed set up a compost heap.

Avoid transplanting sprouts, as it will most likely weaken the sprouts.

Avoid watering plants, as it attracts pests.

Fertilize flowers that no longer bloom.

This is harvest time with ascending forces! Sap is rising, enhancing plant growth above ground, and fruits and vegetables are at their most juicy. Harvest produce is especially suitable for storage.

Gather herbs for vein diseases.

Housework During Waning Moon in Aquarius ☾

The waning moon in Aquarius is best suited for a spring cleaning. Housework is dealt with much more successfully, efficiently, and effortlessly during the waning moon. The cleansing effect on nature extends beyond our bodies into the environment. Problem stains are removed readily. Dirt and pollution are best dealt with during waning moon. Any dirt and spots are removed easily in the laundry, in all areas of house cleaning, at the car wash and in dry cleaning. Reduce on cleaners and save money. Support the environment since waste water is broken down much better.

Clean and store seasonal clothing now.

Thoroughly clean wooden and parquet floors, metals, china, etc.

Cleaning windows and glass is less likely to produce annoying streaks.

Cleaning, polishing, and waterproofing shoes works best.

Combating mold is more effective.

Because Aquarius is linked to the element of air, ventilate rooms thoroughly.

Making preserves yields good results.

It is a good time for baking bread, cakes, and cookies, if more leavening agent is added to the dough.

These are good days for painting.

Nutrition During Waning Moon in Aquarius ☾

During waning moon the body is ready to detox and cleanse, weight gain associated with overeating is less likely. Anybody under weight should consider eating larger portions.

All measures taken to flush out and detoxify the sensitive body parts are very effective. The closer to New Moon the stronger the

impact of the forces. During waning moon any cleansing and detox diets will yield best results. Flush out poisonous substances. Treatment for drug abuse is most effective.

While the moon travels in Aquarius, pay attention to the fats in your diet and to any particularly tempting foods today. Most likely the "wrong" things taste best.

If you have high cholesterol eat a low fat diet.

Include flower vegetables in your meals, as the body digests them very well now.

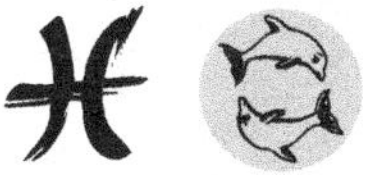

3.12. Moon in Pisces

Element	Plant Part	Gardening	Sensitive Body Parts	Food Component
Water – Wetness	**Leaf**	**Harvest Time**	**Feet and Toes**	**Carbohydrate**

(Chapter 2.1. features the general description of each zodiac sign.)

Success

A time to dismantle the old ahead of building up the new. Sensibility, intuition, and helpfulness are prime. People tend to be more sensible and helpful. Consider that intuition is heightened. This is not the best time for important enterprises. Where possible, retreating is more favorable than dealing with business matters.

Dissolve restrictions, be patient, and wait. Be aware that people can be more easily influenced.

Leisure Time

Your helpfulness will boost friendships. Dancing and swimming are examples of activities you might enjoy the most. It is a time to watch a movie that will inspire your fantasies and imagination.

Instead of big parties you will feel drawn to retreat, relax, and recover.

Romance can be gentle and coziness will prevail.

If you plan outdoor excursions, consider an increased possibility of showers.

☽ Waxing Moon in Pisces

Now is the best time to start anything new or alter, reconfigure, and remodel in many areas such as on the job, at school, for leisure, and in the home. It is essential to focus and gather forces, getting plenty of time to rest, recover, regroup, and gain new strength. The closer it is to Full Moon, the stronger the impact of the forces will be.

♓

Health During Waxing Moon in Pisces ☽

Healing ointments are easily absorbed. All measures taken to supply nutrient materials and strengthen the sensitive body parts of the feet and toes are very effective.

Consider that the nervous system is more sensitive.

Drugs have a much stronger effect on your body. Monitor closely what you put into your body.

Lymphatic therapy is most beneficial.

Close to Full Moon any surgery should be avoided if possible, since the healing process slows down and scarring can be more severe.

Body Care During Waxing Moon in Pisces ☽

All measures taken to supply nutrient materials and strengthen the body are very effective. Treatments with firming and moisturizing creams are more effective as well as massages that serve to regenerate, and strengthen, perhaps with the aid of appropriate oils. Reflexology massage. Carry out any massages with special care, people are more sensitive.

Correcting and cutting ingrown nails during these days promotes healthy growth.

Pamper your feet with a foot bath.

Avoid washing your hair and avoid any haircuts during Pisces days, because hair becomes shaggy and unmanageable and dandruff could develop.

Enjoy the scents of magnolia, amaryllis, and sage.

Garden/Nature During Waxing Moon in Pisces ☽

When the moon travels in Pisces, any garden work benefiting the leaves of a plant is most effective. Sow plants and vegetables that grow below ground, and leaf vegetables.

♓

Transplanting yields good results. Mowing lawns will result in healthy growth.

Avoid pruning fruit trees and bushes.

Water all indoor and outdoor plants. The roots absorb and store more water and as a result will need less frequent watering.

This is harvest time with ascending forces! Sap is rising, enhancing plant growth above ground, and fruits and vegetables are at their most juicy. But harvested produce should be consumed as soon as possible.

Gather herbs for foot complaints.

Housework During Waxing Moon in Pisces ☽

If you intend to remodel or rearrange furniture, start during the waxing moon phase. However, only light housework is advisable, since the waxing moon still requires time to relax, recover, and gather strength.

Because Pisces is linked to the element of water, ventilate rooms briefly and rapidly. Don't air any mattresses.

Any dirt and spots are removed easily in the laundry.

Avoid painting, as paint will take very long to dry.

Preserving and storing should be avoided.

Nutrition During Waxing Moon in Pisces ☽

Everything that is supplied to the body to build up and strengthen is most effective. Stimulants and vitamins have a stronger effect. Any deficiencies of minerals and/or vitamins in the body are best taken care of during the waxing moon. Include all important supplements, tonics, and herbs in your diet. Focus on foods that contain essential minerals and vitamins your body is lacking.

Since the body readily absorbs at this time, you are more likely to gain weight even with a regular amount of food intake. Therefore avoid indulging in rich foods. If you are overweight, eat smaller portions.

Drugs have a much stronger effect. All measures taken to supply nutrient materials and strengthen the sensitive body parts are very effective. Be aware that the body also more readily absorbs poisonous substances. The body retains water more easily, and diuretic measures don't work as effectively.

The body retains water more easily, diuretic measures don't work as effective.

While the moon travels in Pisces, pay attention to the carbohydrates in your diet.

Include leafy vegetables in your meals, as the body digests them very well now.

☾ Waning Moon in Pisces

Now it's time to be active, detoxify, and remove. If your schedule is flexible, plan your activities during the waning moon phase, because you will reach your goals sooner and more easily, yielding better results.

Health During Waning Moon in Pisces ☾

All measures taken to flush out and detoxify the sensitive body parts are very effective. During the waning moon any cleansing and detox diets will yield the best results. Herbal teas, steam room, sauna... anything to detox and cleanse are best utilized between Full Moon and New Moon. The closer to New Moon the stronger the impact of the forces.

The body tends to heal faster during the waning moon and the success rates for surgeries are higher. If you have the choice, schedule surgery, except on the sensitive body parts such as feet and toes, as well as on the respective body parts of the zodiac sign the sun is in. Scarring is less severe, wounds most likely bleed less than during waxing moon, and surgical operations in general are less strenuous on the body. To yield best results schedule dental treatments such as removal of tartar and amalgam as well as fillings, crowns, and dentures.

Blood-purifying and detoxifying herbal infusions and teas are most beneficial.

Consider that the nervous system is more sensitive.

Drugs have a much stronger effect on your body. Monitor closely what you put into your body.

Lymphatic therapy is most beneficial.

Body Care During Waning Moon in Pisces ☾

All measures taken to flush out and detoxify are very effective. The closer to New Moon the stronger the impact of the forces.

Apply detoxing facial and body care, treatments of bumps and pimples on the skin, and exfoliating procedures.

Prepare homemade ointments and cosmetics.

Remove body hair; it won't grow back as quickly. Removal of callused skin works best now.

Correction of the nail bed is advisable. Treatment of obstinate athlete's foot, nail fungus, and warts yields good results.

Massages that serve to relax, ease tension, and detoxify are most effective, such as reflexology massage. Carry out any massages with special care, people are more sensitive.

Pamper your feet with a foot bath.

Avoid washing your hair and avoid any haircuts during Pisces days, because hair becomes shaggy and unmanageable and dandruff could develop.

Enjoy the scents of magnolia, amaryllis, and sage.

Garden/Nature During Waning Moon in Pisces ☾

The waning moon in Pisces favors sowing and planting of plants and vegetables that grow below ground, potatoes, leaf vegetables, and lettuce. Dig over the soil to prepare for planting. Weeding, mowing lawns, and combating pests yields good results.

Water all indoor and outdoor plants. The roots absorb and store more water and as a result will need less frequent watering.

Trimming and cutting back plants will favor healthy growth.

Fertilize flowers. Start a compost heap if needed.

This is harvest time with ascending forces! Sap is rising, enhancing plant growth above ground, and fruits and vegetables are at their most juicy. But harvested produce should be consumed as soon as possible.

Gather herbs for foot complaints.

Housework During Waning Moon in Pisces ☾

Housework is dealt with much more successfully, efficiently, and effortlessly during the waning moon. The cleansing effect on nature extends beyond our bodies into the environment. Problem stains are removed readily. Dirt and pollution are best dealt with during waning moon. Any dirt and spots are removed easily in the laundry, in all areas of house cleaning, at the car wash and in dry cleaning. Reduce on cleaners and save money. Support the environment since waste water is broken down much better.

Thoroughly clean wooden and parquet floors, metals, china, etc.

Cleaning, polishing, and waterproofing shoes works best.

Combating mold is more effective. Clean and store seasonal clothing.

Because Pisces is linked to the element of water, ventilate rooms briefly and rapidly. Don't air any mattresses.

Avoid painting, as paint will take very long to dry.

Preserving and storing should be avoided.

Nutrition During Waning Moon in Pisces ☾

During waning moon the body is ready to detoxify and cleanse, and weight gain associated with overeating is less likely. Anybody underweight should consider eating larger portions.

All measures taken to flush out and detoxify the sensitive body parts are very effective. The closer to New Moon the stronger the impact of the forces. During the waning moon any cleansing and detox diets will yield the best results. Flush out poisonous substances. Treatment for drug abuse is most effective.

Caffeine, alcohol, drugs, certain foods, and stimulants have a much stronger effect!

While the moon travels in Pisces, pay attention to the carbohydrates in your diet.

Include leafy vegetables in your meals, as the body digests them very well now.

Notes

1 *https://www.wildlife.ca.gov/Fishing/Ocean/Grunion*

2 *https://asknature.org/strategy/lunar-cycle-triggers-reproduction/#.WmI9-jdryM9*

3 *https://www.sciencedaily.com/releases/2005/08/050802064144.htm*

4 *Au, F. von: Der große Aussaat-Kalender, Der richtige Zeitpunkt für Aussaat, Vermehrung und Pflege im Zeichen des wechselnden Mondes, München 1996*
Elmadfa, I./Aign, W./Fritzsche, D.: GU Kompaß Nährwerte, München 1997
Graf, C.: Gärtnern mit dem Mond, München 1994
Graf, C.: Kochen mit dem Mond, München 1995
Paungger, J./Poppe, T.: Vom richtigen Zeitpunkt, Die Anwendung des Mondkalenders im täglichen Leben, München 1991
Paungger, J./Poppe, T.: Aus eigener Kraft, Gesundsein und Gesundwerden in Harmonie mit Natur- und Mondrhythmen, München 1996
Edith Stadig: Mein Leben mit dem Mondrhythmus, Der Kalender, Clebitady Verlag, Rutesheim 2016
Edith Stadig: Besser Leben mit dem Mondrhythmus, Der praktische Ratgeber, Clebitady Verlag, Rutesheim 2011

37124224R00086

Made in the USA
Middletown, DE
23 February 2019